lonely planet KIDS

AMERICA'S
NATIONAL PARKS

written by
ALEXA WARD

illustrated by
MIKE LOWERY

CONTENTS

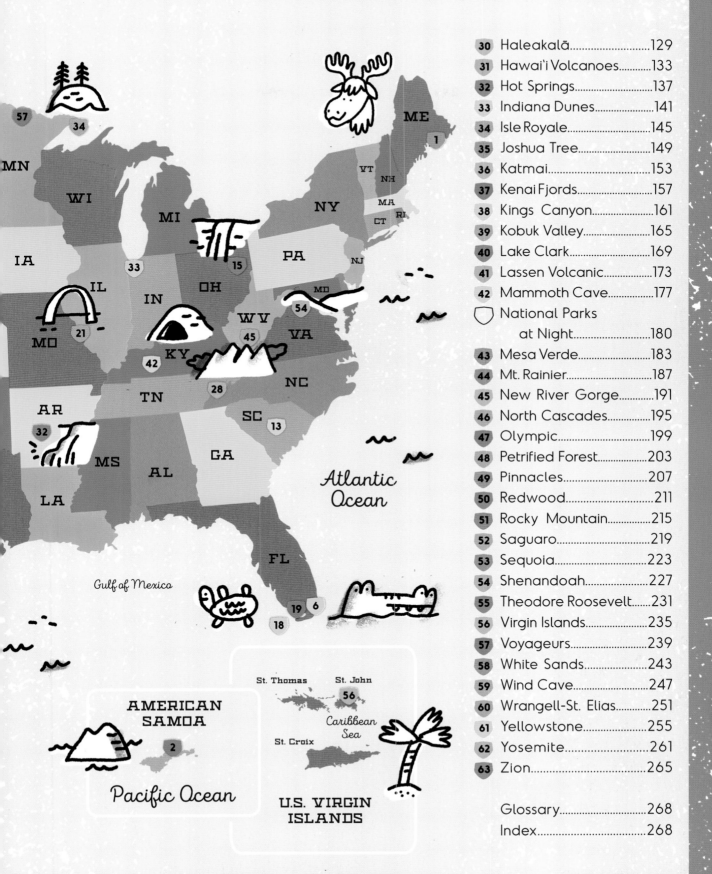

INTRODUCTION

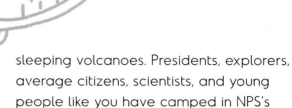

Everyone is a little bit wild—including you. Whether you live in a big city or a tiny suburb or somewhere in between, you've probably splashed in puddles after your parents told you not to, or stared out your classroom window at a squirrel bouncing along a power line. I bet you've howled at the moon once or twice when no one was around. If you've ever traveled to a national park, you know that America is a little bit wild, too. In fact, it's a lot wild.

America's national parks are bursting with gasp-worthy wonders: the world's largest tree, with branches that stretch almost 400 feet into the sky; the planet's grandest canyon, whose gold-and-red cliffs plummet 6,000 feet down; a crystal-clear lake that is deep enough to swallow the Empire State Building. Each one is unique, but together, these world-famous parks tell a story of wilderness, adventure, and exploration—a tale that is woven into all of nature. President Woodrow Wilson created the National Park Service (NPS) on August 25, 1916, but the fight to protect and preserve the country's most amazing wild spaces began around 1860. Since then, millions of people from all over the world have walked the paths of all 63 parks in the NPS. Before that (and still today), Native American tribes like the Crow and the Cheyenne hunted bison in the shadows of sleeping volcanoes. Presidents, explorers, average citizens, scientists, and young people like you have camped in NPS's forests and fields, under the same blanket of stars. Now, it's your turn!

Whether you're lucky enough to have a park on your doorstep or need to take a car, bus, train, or plane to visit one, we hope that this guide transports you to the wolf-howling, water-rushing, heart-racing, lava-exploding, incredibly exciting, and unbelievably *real* world of America's national parks. Let the photos of rocky spires and roaring bears fill your daydreams. Close your eyes and imagine a brisk mountain wind or the heat of a crackling campfire on your face. The facts in these pages are only the beginning of what you will discover when you study our native wilderness. There's only one rule for enjoying this book—have a blast!

WELL, WHAT ARE YOU WAITING FOR?! TURN THE PAGE ALREADY. AN ADVENTURE IS WAITING FOR YOU!

SAFETY & RESPONSIBILITY

Visiting a national park can be the experience of a lifetime, but not if you damage the park or get hurt. Luckily, we have a strategy for keeping you safe and happy in America's wildlands: follow the **S.T.A.R.S.**

 **S** **tick to the path.** While it may seem fun to wander into the forest or explore on your own, don't. There are many dangers hiding just off the walking trail. Loose rocks. Steep cliffs. Boiling hot springs. Yikes! Rangers work hard to keep paths safe so you can enjoy wild nature without getting lost or injured.

 T **ake in, take out.** Sadly, many people leave trash behind in parks. Litter not only looks ugly—it can also harm wildlife. Please pick up after yourself. This is way more important than cleaning your room!

 A **dmire, but don't touch.** Don't remove natural objects (sticks, stones, or artifacts) from the park. You don't like it when people mess with your stuff, right?

 R **espect wildlife.** These animals are called "wild" for a reason—they are *not* pets. Never approach an animal. Instead, use a camera or binoculars to get a better view. Following this guideline will keep you *and* the animals safe and healthy.

 S **tay hydrated.** Exploring a national park is hard work! Drink lots of water and wear plenty of sunscreen. This is extra important if you are visiting a park in extremely hot or cold temperatures.

Park in Numbers

74
Area covered (sq miles)

1,530
Highest point:
Cadillac Mountain (ft)

50+
Miles of shoreline

ME

ACADIA NATIONAL PARK

You'll feel like a peregrine falcon as you perch atop Acadia's seaside peaks while the rough ocean tides churn over a thousand feet below you. This park is nestled at the easternmost tip of the continental United States. At its highest point, the summit of Cadillac Mountain, you get a bird's-eye view of the coastal landscape.

PICTURE THIS:

Your feet are dangling over a giant granite boulder that sits near the edge of a cliff. The sounds of water crashing against rocks gets louder around you, filling the air like music. As the sun rises, the dark sky blazes with a streak of red, then turns pink and orange and purple, until all the colors seep over the horizon as quickly as sherbet melts on a summer day. Far below, you watch the black waves grow blue. Welcome to Cadillac Mountain in Acadia National Park on the coast of Maine, the first place where the sun rises in the United States from October to March.

But if you'd rather *not* wake up at the crack of dawn, there's still plenty to do in Acadia—activities that you might not expect in a national park. For example, if you want to take a break from the rugged outdoors, you can drink tea on the rolling green lawns of Jordan Pond House. Or perhaps you'd like a horse-drawn carriage ride instead? Well, you're in luck: the park has 45 miles of carriage-friendly roads dotted with fancy cottages and cozy inns. More than 100 years ago, Acadia drew the richest people in America to its rocky shores, and though the land became a national park in 1919, hints of their lavish lifestyle remain to this day.

📷 *Main images: Park coastline (below); cliffs in Acadia National Park (opposite). Snapshots from top: Fiery sunrise; one of the most photographed bridges in Acadia National Park.*

THINGS to SEE

Peregrine Falcons: Diving at speeds of over 200 miles per hour, this falcon species clocks in as the fastest animal on the planet. Find them nesting in the park during springtime.

Tide Pools: Colorful starfish, crabby crustaceans, and delicate sponges lounge in the pools of seawater that speckle Acadia's shoreline. It's like wildlife soup!

Aside from the steaming tea and fine horses, the park is absolutely wild. Dense forests curl up around wet, boggy marshes. In winter, blankets of snow make for ideal cross-country skiing. With over 50 miles of craggy shoreline, Acadia offers wonder for everyone.

THINGS to DO

Mountain Summiting: If you can't hike to the top of Cadillac Mountain, don't worry—you can drive the 3.5-mile road to the top. But bundle up! It's cold and windy up there.

Whale Watching: During summer or fall, hop on a whale-watching boat from the town of Bar Harbor. You might spot minke, fin, and even humpback whales playing in the chilly waters.

Park *in* Numbers

21.1
Area in sq miles—about one-third
of which is underwater

3,000
Years of Samoan settlement

3,170
Highest point: Lata Mountain (ft)

WELCOME!

02

AS

NATIONAL PARK OF AMERICAN SAMOA

The excitement to be had south of the equator on this group of islands—sandy beaches, coral reefs, and an extraordinary culture—will make you never want to leave this faraway paradise, part of which is underwater.

national Park of American Samoa is no exception. Positioned 2,600 miles southwest of Hawai'i (4,700 miles from California), this park is a tiny dot in the giant blue Pacific Ocean. Being in the middle of the sea has its advantages—unique wildlife thrive in its cloud forests on its volcanic peaks, and in its waters (there are 950 species of fish here).

The islands' culture is even more distinctive than its animals and plants. In this far-flung land, you can immerse yourself in the 3,000-year-old traditions of Polynesia's oldest surviving culture. If you think we're trying to give you homework, you're wrong. Samoan history isn't recorded in books—instead, beliefs, traditions, and myths are kept alive through storytelling.

Though the tale of how this park was established is still a mystery, we know for a fact that Samoan chiefs allowed sections of the islands of Tutuila, Ofu, and Ta'ū to be opened as national parks in 1993. The chiefs, who have guarded the islands for thousands of years, expanded the park in 2002 to include Olosega island. You're welcome!

📷 Main images:
A beach in American
Samoa (below left);
Fatu Rock, or the Flower Pot
Rock, in Pago Pago Habor
(right). Snapshots from top:
Antler coral; flying foxes,
also known as fruit bats.

THINGS to SEE

Samoan Flying Foxes: These bats are native to American Samoa, Samoa, and its island neighbor, Fiji. They can't be found anywhere else in the world! Like bees, they pollinate flowers and other plants.

Antler Coral: This stony coral owes its wild colors to the microscopic marine plants called zooxanthellae that live inside it. Try saying that five times fast!

THINGS to DO

Go Snorkeling: You can't visit the park without getting a front-row view of its spectacular underwater life. Here, there are more fish than people!

Ride the Bus: No, really—hop on one of the many brightly painted buses that zigzag through the forests and curve along the palm-lined coast.

Park in Numbers

119.6
Area covered (sq miles)

3,600
Weight of Balanced Rock (tons)

2,000+
Natural stone arches

03
UT
ARCHES
NATIONAL
PARK

The Arch. This epic structure stands tall, rising above its vast desert kingdom like the legs of an ancient giant. As you look toward the horizon, more than 2,000 of these natural sandstone behemoths rise up to greet you, while foxes and bobcats play at their base. Watch as the arches' colors and shapes change in the sun—or is it only a mirage?

"REACH FOR THE SKY!"

f the humongous red rock formations in Arches National Park could speak, that's exactly what they'd tell you. From a distance, the landscape looks like it was built inside your favorite video game. Large orange blocks of stone were plunked down seemingly at random on a field of sand. Spiky rocks are scattered over the ground, as if a mythological beast left its dentures there. But when you get really close to the arches, pillars, and fairy chimneys (tall, spindly rock towers) in this national park, you'll discover something even more surprising than the formations themselves: it looks as if they're about to crumble into dust. Balanced Rock, a massive rock that weighs about as much as 17 blue whales, seems to teeter back and forth. Watching it hover more than 50 feet in the air will make your heart race.

Arches National Park's odd features didn't just *happen*. Sixty-five million years ago, geological forces—Earth's superpowers—squeezed flat rock into folds as tight as an accordion's. Eventually, the pressure in the folds caused the rock to crack like an egg. Then, a huge uplift punched the landmass skyward, making the sandstone split all over again. Over the following millions and millions of years, water wore down the sandstone little by little in a process called **erosion**. Ice fractured solid slabs, forming narrow passageways in the rock, while waterways sculpted more of the amazing shapes you see today. In other words, this national park is an art project made by nature itself. We give it an A+!

📷 *Main images: Delicate Arch at sunset (above); faded rattlesnake (right); Turret Arch through the North Window (top right). Snapshots from top: Petroglyphs; sunset over Arches.*

THINGS to SEE

Petroglyphs: Horse and rider. Doglike creatures. Bighorn sheep. Members of the Ute tribe etched these shapes into the rock face hundreds of years ago. For many Native Americans today, the images are an important connection to their ancestors who created them.

Midget Faded Rattlesnakes: The pattern on this snake's back resembles faded drops of blood. Take that as a warning to stay away from its highly toxic venom! Luckily, this deadly rattler is mostly active at night. If you do see one of these vipers, remain at a distance.

THINGS to DO

Hiking: People often call Arches an outdoor playground. The best way to experience it is to hike through its mesmerizing stone clusters. We recommend the ranger-led excursion to Fiery Furnace—a maze of red rocks that cuts through the heart of the park.

White-Water Rafting: Looking for a little more adventure? Crash and splash your way along the Colorado River, which rushes along the southern border of the park . . . but *only* with the permission of an adult. An added bonus: wildlife spotting.

Park *in* Numbers

381
Area covered (sq miles)

1
Annual landscape erosion (in)

3,340
Highest point (ft)

EERIE, RIGHT?

04

SD

BADLANDS NATIONAL PARK

A quiet buzz of excitement, mystery, and wonder sends sparks racing over your skin. This is what it feels like to step into the Badlands. Entering this barren landscape is as magical as opening a door into another world, or setting foot on an alien planet. Just remember . . . it's not as empty as it seems.

That's why in the 1900s, French fur trappers said that this region had bad lands to pass through. Even the native Lakota called it Makhóšiča, or "bad land." Everyone agrees: there's something eerie about this place. Maybe the park's extreme temperatures and lack of water give people the heebie-jeebies. Or maybe it's the crinkly rock outcroppings that give so many visitors goose bumps . . .

But some say that hiking the Badlands feels like walking on the moon, and a stroll in outer space sounds awesome. So why not give the Badlands a try? The longer you explore, the more you'll see. It's like scouring a puzzle for clues, or letting your eyes adjust to the dark. That bare field of grass? That's actually a **prairie** teeming with animal activity. Those plain old rocks? They're crawling with life—and evidence of past life. The Badlands hold one of the richest fossil beds in the entire world. Why walk on the moon when you can walk with prehistoric beasts?

WANNA BUTT HEADS?

📷 *Main image: Eroded rock formations. Snapshots from top: Milky Way over the Badlands; Rocky Mountain bighorn sheep; turkey vulture.*

THE BADLANDS ARE KIND OF CREEPY.

THINGS to SEE

Bighorn Sheep: These sheep can be hard to spot because of their camouflage. If you do see one, remember that their sturdy horns aren't for show. They're for epic head-butt battles.

Turkey Vultures: The wrinkled red and pink face of this large bird looks like a Halloween mask. Instead of candy, these harmless buzzards dine mainly on carrion—animals that have recently died. "Bone" appétit!

THINGS to DO

Hunt for Fossils: Stop by the Fossil Preparation Lab, then grab a fossil-recording form at the visitor center. Use it to report any fossils you spot. Once, a seven-year-old girl found a saber-toothed cat skull! Just remember: admire, but don't touch!

Stargazing: The big open spaces. The lack of light pollution. You've never seen the night sky sparkle like this. A ranger will even lend you their telescope to see the Milky Way.

I'M NOT CREEPY. YOU'RE CREEPY.

Park in Numbers

1,252
Area covered (sq miles)

7,832
Highest point (ft)

1,295
Number of plant species

05

TX

BIG BEND NATIONAL PARK

In the scorching heart of the desert, way out in a far-flung corner of Texas, a hidden oasis awaits hikers, backpackers, and nature lovers—if only you stop long enough to discover its dust-covered wonders.

ig Bend National Park is *hot, hot, hot*. Summer temperatures often climb higher than 100°F. In the shimmering heat of the Chihuahuan Desert, Big Bend resembles a barren wasteland— at first. But amid its steep canyons and desert scrubland, you'll find plenty of water in the Rio Grande, which forms the southern border of the park. And where there's water, there's life: stubborn cacti, shy tarantulas, and piglike mammals called javelinas are only a few examples of the wildlife hiding in this dust-blown domain. There are more recorded bird species in Big Bend than in any other national park in America. Now, that's a hoot!

This park is a seven-layer cake of geological history. Its landscape is a mix of 100-million-year-old rocks and newer sand dunes that are still being carved and eroded by the hot desert winds that whip against your face. Because the area looks so dry, it's difficult to imagine that Big Bend once lay beneath an ancient tropical sea brimming with ferocious, sharp-toothed marine life, but the fossil record doesn't lie. Among the fossilized treasures discovered here is the skull of a three-horned *Chasmosaurus*, an ancient species distantly related to the *Triceratops*.

Big Bend is an important record of human life, too. Artifacts from Paleo-Indians that lived in the region date back 10,000 years. Later, groups like the Chisos tribe, along with Spanish colonizers, had a presence on the land. Ranchers, miners, revolutionaries, pioneers, and even criminal outlaws passed through Big Bend. Explorers—like you—crossed the Rio Grande, searching for gold and silver.

Main images: The Rio Grande (opposite); an abandoned post office (below). Snapshots clockwise from top: Yucca tree at the side of a road; a coyote crosses the street.

THINGS to SEE

Texas Brown Tarantulas: Covered in hair and as large as a mouse, tarantulas look frightening, but they wouldn't hurt a fly. Well, okay, they would eat a fly, but they're not a threat to humans.

Giant Swallowtail Butterflies: These enormous butterflies are the largest species in North America. They have a wingspan of up to 6 inches. That's bigger than your hand!

THINGS to DO

Bird-watching: Big Bend is home to over 450 bird species. In the Rio Grande Village alone, you can see herons, ducks, kingfishers, white-winged doves, vermilion flycatchers, and Cooper's hawks.

Ghost Town Tourism: If you like a good shiver up your spine, mosey on over to the ghost town Terlingua, where you can walk among the ruins of old buildings and a cemetery. Yeehaw!

Park *in* Numbers

270.3
Area covered (sq miles)

50+
Number of documented wrecks
within the park's boundaries

10,000
Years that humans have been
active in the park area

FL

BISCAYNE NATIONAL PARK

Haunted by ghostly shipwrecks and teeming with sea turtles and larger-than-life manatees, this sunken jewel of the national park system is a paradise for explorers and deep-sea adventurers.

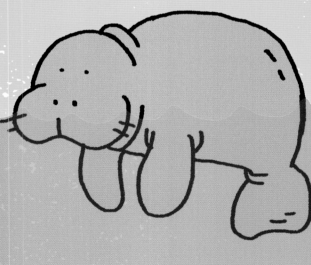

If you've ever dreamed of becoming a pirate, a sailor, or a mermaid, put Biscayne National Park at the top of your list. This underwater playground has nurtured human life for over 10,000 years—including indigenous tribes, Spanish conquistadors, pineapple farmers, and plundering pirates. Now it's your turn to venture among the sandy beaches and splash in the shockingly blue seascape that makes up 95% of this national park.

THINGS to SEE

Spiny Lobsters: When scared, these clawless creatures—which are not as closely related to lobsters as you might think—"screech" by rubbing their antennae against their exoskeleton. *La la la laaaaa!*

Florida Manatees: Ah, the cows of the sea! Scientists theorize that these gentle giants evolved from land mammals. Did you know that manatees are the inspiration for mermaid myths?

THINGS to DO

Snorkeling: The only way to *really* explore Biscayne is to become a fish. So pop on your snorkel, mask, and fins to view more than 600 different marine species as you bob above shallow-water shipwrecks.

Canoeing and Kayaking: If swimming's not your thing, go on a paddle-powered adventure around Biscayne's channels, creeks, and lagoons. There are plenty of turtles, dolphins, and manatees to spot in the turquoise water.

Though there are countless stories buried in this sunken kingdom, one is known to all: people have fought to conserve this land for hundreds of years. Thankfully, Biscayne officially became part of the NPS in 1968. Now, its four unique **ecosystems**—mangrove forests, islands, bay, and coral reef—are protected.

And thank goodness, because its **biodiversity** will blow your mind. More than 50 kinds of crustacea, more than 600 species of fish, and more than 25 types of mammals live here. American crocodiles, giant blue land crabs, rattlesnakes, and reef octopuses make Biscayne home. To date, 44 shipwrecks have been discovered in this wonderland beneath the sea.

Even though you can see the city of Miami from the shoreline, the islands are a different world. If you don't like roughing it, Biscayne might not be for you. But if you do, prepare to camp under the stars!

📷 *Main images: Fowey Rocks Lighthouse (top); a manatee (middle); roseate spoonbills (bottom).*

DON'T LOOK DOWN!

Just kidding! Looking down is the whole point of visiting Black Canyon of the Gunnison. But be warned that a peek over the edge might make your stomach flip. At more than 2,000 feet, it's one of the deepest canyons in the country.

This park is extreme—only experts can scale these walls of rock, while kayaking the dangerous rapids of the Gunnison River is best left to the professionals. However, there's still plenty to see: the views of the canyon itself are worth the trip. The clear, greenish waters of the river are unlike anything else in the country.

 *Main image: Black Canyon of the Gunnison. Snapshots from top: A chipmunk on the bank of the Gunnison River; a twisted juniper tree.*

THINGS to SEE

Mule Deer: These long-eared deer are all over the park. Look for their adorable spotted fawns early in summer.

Great Horned Owls: With a five-foot wingspan, these are one of America's largest owls. They hunt along the canyon rim, under the cover of night.

THINGS to DO

Hike the Trails: As you descend to the bottom of the canyon, keep an eye out for the marble-striped Painted Wall, Colorado's tallest cliff.

Horseback Riding: The park's only horse trail is on the North Rim, a dizzying sight that will take your breath away. Howdy, partner!

Park *in* Numbers

52
Area covered (sq miles)

9,115
Highest point:
Rainbow Point (ft)

600+
Endangered Utah prairie dogs

UT

BRYCE CANYON NATIONAL PARK

Walking through the rock spires, slim canyons, and curved arches of this park feels like being inside a colorful dream. Here, you can become the ruler of your own fantasy world by exploring one of the unique, castle-like mesas or fortresses of limestone.

MAGIC.

There's no other word to describe the melting colors and bizarre geological features you'll find in Bryce Canyon National Park in Southwestern Utah. If you enjoy daydreaming or painting, the landscape will stir your imagination to new heights. Even reading the list of sights—Wall of Windows, Thor's Hammer, Fairyland Point, and Silent City—is like flipping through the pages of an adventure book. Like other parks in the area, the unique shape of Bryce was formed primarily by the power of water: ice, frost, and rainwater sculpted the park in ways no artist could.

Bryce is a trip backward in time, too— some of the trees here are thousands of years old. Plus, its night skies are so clear, you can see all the way to the Andromeda galaxy. That's 2.2 million light-years away! The ancient-looking vistas make it easy to picture the Paleo-Indians who hunted large mammals here, under the same stars, at the end of the last ice age.

THINGS to SEE

Utah Prairie Dogs: These highly social animals once dominated the Southwest by the millions. Now endangered, the population in Bryce Canyon resulted from the effort to protect these adorable rodents.

Ponderosa Pines: Though impossible to climb, these huge pines are very useful. Native Americans ate their seeds and used their "pitch," or resin, to waterproof canoes and tents.

THINGS to DO

Bryce Point: This perch offers a view of the Silent City, a forest of **hoodoos** that look like a cityscape on Mars. At sunset, it's easy to pretend that you're on an alien planet.

Stargazing: You've never seen the Milky Way as clearly as you will on a moonless night at Bryce. Stargazers from all over the world descend upon the park for a four-day festival every summer.

📷 *Main images: Bryce Canyon National Park (opposite); a Utah prairie dog (silhouette); the Milky Way (below); a ponderosa pine cone (above). Snapshot: The ponderosa pine forests of the Paunsaugunt Plateau.*

Park in Numbers

527
Area covered (sq miles)

350
Bighorn sheep

7,120
Highest point: Cathedral Point,
Needles District (ft)

09

UT

CANYON-LANDS NATIONAL PARK

Mighty rivers carved this plateau into a maze of soaring mesas, crumbling spires, and arches that resemble your favorite roller coaster.

Y ou'll find this park inside the Colorado Plateau, a 150,580-square-mile table of layered rocks that has been forming for millions of years. Though water shaped the spires, arches, and sandstone bridges, the Canyonlands gets less than 10 inches of rain per year. The wide range of resident desert animals—mountain lions, bobcats, snakes, and even bears—fight for survival in the high desert.

The Colorado and the Green Rivers form a Y that cuts the land into three separate zones, each with its own special features. One is the Island in the Sky District, which lures travelers with overlooks so high, they make you feel like you're about to launch into outer space. Not far from there is a spellbinding place called the Needles, where you can camp at the feet of giant sandstone spires. There are plenty of short hikes here, too—check out the Cave Spring Loop, which leads to an abandoned cowboy camp, in addition to pictographs left behind by hunter-gatherers over 10,000 years ago.

No matter where you go, there's one sight you can't miss: the night sky. Declared an International Dark Sky Park in 2015, the Canyonlands is one of the best places in the world to stargaze.

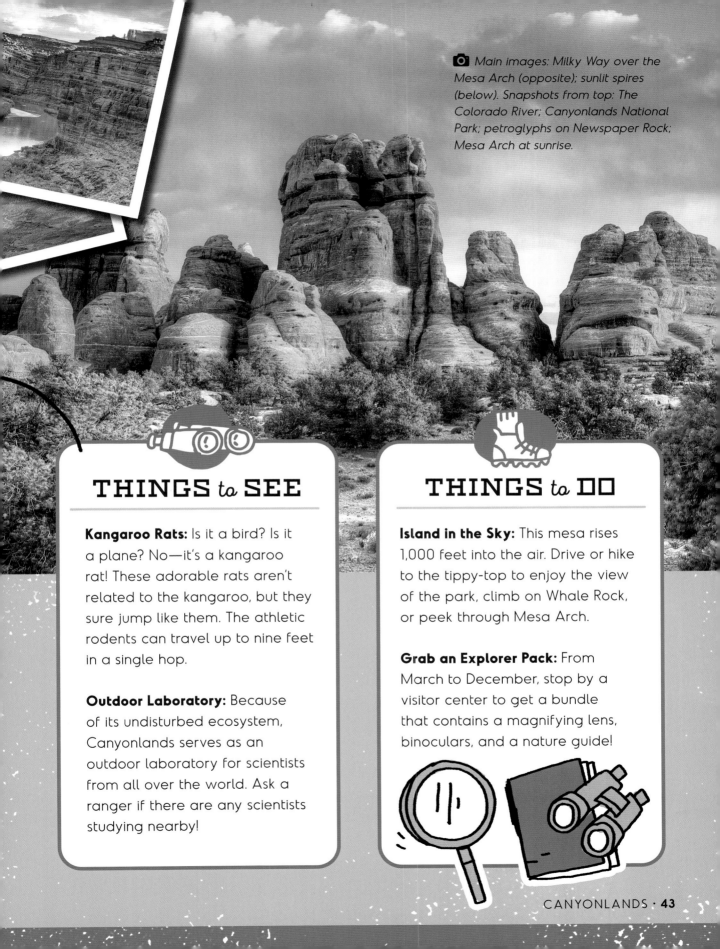

📷 *Main images: Milky Way over the Mesa Arch (opposite); sunlit spires (below). Snapshots from top: The Colorado River; Canyonlands National Park; petroglyphs on Newspaper Rock; Mesa Arch at sunrise.*

THINGS to SEE

Kangaroo Rats: Is it a bird? Is it a plane? No—it's a kangaroo rat! These adorable rats aren't related to the kangaroo, but they sure jump like them. The athletic rodents can travel up to nine feet in a single hop.

Outdoor Laboratory: Because of its undisturbed ecosystem, Canyonlands serves as an outdoor laboratory for scientists from all over the world. Ask a ranger if there are any scientists studying nearby!

THINGS to DO

Island in the Sky: This mesa rises 1,000 feet into the air. Drive or hike to the tippy-top to enjoy the view of the park, climb on Whale Rock, or peek through Mesa Arch.

Grab an Explorer Pack: From March to December, stop by a visitor center to get a bundle that contains a magnifying lens, binoculars, and a nature guide!

10

UT

CAPITOL REEF NATIONAL PARK

You've probably never heard of this national park, so shhhhh—it's one of the National Park Service's best-kept secrets.

📷 *Main image: Scenic Route 24. Snapshots from top: Historic barn in Capitol Reef; a golden eagle.*

*L*ike Canyonlands and Arches, Capitol Reef is one of Utah's many weird and wonderful national parks made up of red arches, stone domes, and canyons the color of wet clay. The park comprises a giant wrinkle in the earth known as Waterpocket Fold, formed about 50 million years ago, when the ground folded over itself for a stretch of 100 miles.

Despite its name, you won't find any coral, fish, or scuba divers. The "reef" in Capitol Reef refers to the park's rocky cliffs. The spiky, jagged terrain halted early settlers in their tracks as they attempted to cross the country. Imagine that traffic jam!

The geography of Capitol Reef is confusing, and so mazelike that a very famous bank robber named Butch Cassidy once used the park as his secret hideout. But you don't have to break the law to enjoy this desert "reef." Visitors love to explore the park's winding paths and gawk at its ancient rock art. Though the pioneers rode through this extremely rough terrain in covered wagons, you'll see current-day tourists buzzing along in gas-guzzling vehicles.

Scientists have discovered that this area contains some of the oldest reptile tracks in the Western Hemisphere. These animals roamed the earth *before the dinosaurs*. That's canyon country, ya varmints!

THINGS to SEE

Long-Nosed Leopard Lizards: What a tongue twister! Named for their multicolored spots, these reptiles love to run in wide-open spaces, often with their forelimbs in the air. Hands up!

Golden Eagles: With regal, golden neck feathers and a wingspan of up to seven feet, these eagles are lightning quick. Golden eagles swoop down from the cliffs to pick off rabbits and marmots.

THINGS to DO

Experience Settler Life: Though Mormon settlers left long ago, the apricot, cherry, peach, pear, and apple trees they planted remain. Pick seasonal fruit alongside local wildlife, like yellow-bellied marmots.

Grand Wash: This canyon grows narrower and narrower as you walk through the Creamsicle-striped corridor. Lounge in the crevices and natural pockets that dot the sandstone walls.

Park in Numbers

73
Area covered (sq miles)

1,604
Deepest point (ft)

120
Known caves

11

NM

CARLSBAD CAVERNS NATIONAL PARK

If you lose yourself inside the pages of fantasy novels, you'll fall in love with these very real subterranean tunnels, which are as magical as any hidden realm.

WANT TO HUNT FOR BURIED TREASURE?

Just beneath the cactus-covered ridges of the soaring Guadalupe Mountains in New Mexico, the **arid** desert air smacks against a set of chillingly cool, eerily silent tunnels under the earth. You don't need a map: the change in temperature is as good as an X marking the spot.

THINGS to SEE

Giant Desert Centipedes: These creepy-crawlies can grow up to eight inches long. Careful— they have a nasty sting.

Cave Pearls: These calcite "jewels" developed as layers of calcite built up around a grain of sand. If taken outside the caverns, they would crumble to dust.

THINGS to DO

Bats, Man!: From April to mid-October, you can watch an army of Brazilian free-tailed bats flow out of the cave at dusk. Over 400,000 of these winged creatures roost in the caves.

King's Palace: A ranger-led tour to these four underground chambers is a quest to the park's deepest, darkest caverns.

📷 *Main images: Subterranean columns in spring-fed pool (top); cave entrance (middle); a bat (bottom). Snapshot: Giant desert centipede.*

Here, a museum of geological formations awaits you around every corner. Even their scientific names—stalactites, stalagmites, helictites—conjure images of wizard-worthy spells. A shallow sea covered this area 265 million years ago. But as the earth changed—as all organic life tends to—an underwater reef was buried under deposits of minerals like salt and gypsum. Then, like a mythical sea god, the ancient reef rose two miles into the sky. As rainwater seeped into the resulting cracks, fresh water mixed with hydrogen sulfide to create sulfuric acid, which slowly melted the passages into the rock. Now, they are here to explore.

Native Americans in the area knew of these caves for hundreds or even thousands of years, but it is not clear that they explored deep inside. In 1898, a teenager named Jim White wandered into a cave by accident. Like an adventurer in a book, he gave many of the rooms and formations the incredible names they inspire, such as King's Palace, Bottomless Pit, and Witch's Finger.

Park *in* Numbers

390
Area covered (sq miles)

5
Islands

145
Species found nowhere
else in the world

12

CA

CHANNEL ISLANDS NATIONAL PARK

If you've ever dreamed of sailing to the ends of the earth on a high-seas adventure, look no further than this necklace of islands off the coast of California, where wildlife flourishes like a garden in summertime.

Channel Islands National Park is also called the Galápagos of North America, and—trust us—the islands have earned their nickname. Like the Galápagos, where the theory of evolution took root in the 19th century, many of the animals and plants on the Channel Islands are **endemic**, which means that they exist nowhere else in the world. Left alone on this remote land, animals such as gigantic northern elephant seals, northern fur seals, island foxes, and island night lizards evolved here, developing unique features over time. The Channel Islands are a secluded paradise where wildlife can evolve in peace!

Each of the park's five islands is special. Anacapa, closest to mainland California, is made up of three tiny islets. During spring, thousands of nesting seabirds blanket the ground with their feathers. Santa Cruz is home to Diablo Peak, a 2,450-foot-high mountain, and Painted Cave, which is one of the largest sea caves in the world! If you want to delve into a more prehistoric past, Santa Rosa, the second-largest island, has tons of archaeological sites and fossil finds. Did you know that miniature mammoths called pygmy mammoths once trumpeted over the islands? Their ancestors swam from the mainland and loved the islands so much that they decided to stay!

THINGS *to* SEE

Northern Elephant Seals: Once on the verge of extinction, these hulking beasts—19th-century explorers called them "sea bears"—are now thriving on the islands due to conservation efforts.

Island Foxes: Like elephant seals, these tiny canids (part of the dog family) nearly went extinct. The Chumash hold native foxes in high regard as pets of the sun or dream helpers.

THINGS *to* DO

Kayaking: Paddle your kayak (with an adult) through the crystal-blue waters along the shoreline, under sea arches and towering cliffs, to explore the islands' many spooky sea caves.

Explore Tide Pools: Around every island's shoreline, these rocky pools hold a rainbow of brightly colored marine critters, including sea stars, spiny urchins, and tiny periwinkle snails.

📷 *Main images: Pierced rock near Anacapa Island (opposite); a northern elephant seal (above, silhouette). Snapshots left to right: A young California sea lion; an anemone glows under the sun's rays; prickly pear cactus; an island fox; the coast of Santa Cruz Island.*

When you step onto the lonely, windy bluffs, it's hard to believe that any humans lived here—but where there's a will, there's a way. The Chumash tribespeople arrived 13,000 years ago in *tomols* (canoes carved out of redwood logs) to build villages. Much later, European explorers, seal and abalone hunters, livestock ranchers, and even smugglers landed on the rocky shores as well. After centuries of human activity and pollution threatening wildlife—humans can be the worst sometimes—the islands are now in recovery, thanks to **conservation** projects led by scientists and activists.

Park in Numbers

41.7
Area covered (sq miles)

170
Height of tallest tree (ft)

0
Park entrance fee ($)

13

SC

CONGAREE NATIONAL PARK

Dip your oar into the black waters of the Congaree, where you'll experience muffled cries of birds in the distance, insects buzzing in your ear, and a jungle of gangly trees looming overhead as you journey into a land with South Carolina's finest mud, moss, and marvels.

"**Old-growth forest**" refers to trees that have remained safe from wildfire, insect infestations, and other woodsy catastrophes (think of them as the great-grandparents of the tree world). Here, you'll find a fairyland of ancient, gnarly, alien-like "Groots": bald cypresses with skirted bottoms, swamp tupelos jeweled with emerald-colored lichen, and water hickories with strips of bark peeling like wallpaper in a haunted mansion.

Okay, technically, Congaree is not a swamp—it's a forest floodplain. But it is swampy. The Congaree River forms the southern border of the park. Its waters jump with fish, turtles, and snakes. These dark swamps are like something out of a book—look out for lurking reptiles, amphibians, insects, and birds, as well as feral pigs. Bring your bug spray!

This land cannot be tamed. When European colonizers tried to farm the swamp, floods washed away their crops over and over again. Eventually, loggers moved in and began to chop down the bald cypress trees for lumber . . . but this proved difficult, too. The land is so boggy that the felled trees would get stuck in the soupy water. Now, thanks to environmentalists, Congaree received national park status in 2003. Party on,

📷 *Main images: Boardwalk at Congaree (left); swampland at Congaree (right). Snapshots top to bottom: Golden orb spider; bracket fungi on a fallen tree limb; a rotting cypress in the swamp.*

THINGS to SEE

wading birds, and reptiles.

Spanish Moss: This plant—which is more closely related to pineapples than moss—dangles from the tree branches like holiday decorations or Rapunzel's long hair.

Eastern Box Turtles: The name "box" turtle comes from this orange-and-black reptile's ability to withdraw completely into its shell. Take that, Optimus Prime!

THINGS to DO

swamp—er, swamp*ish*—lovers!

Canoeing: Paddling through the primeval old-growth forest is the experience of a lifetime. See otters, turtles, snakes, and salamanders as you float past knobby bald cypress trees.

Nature Walks: Throughout the year, you can join a volunteer nature guide for a stroll along Congaree's boardwalks, where you'll learn about swamp plants,

Park in Numbers

286
Area covered (sq miles)

5
Volume of water in the lake
(trillion gallons)

4,800
Years since most recent eruption

14

OR

CRATER LAKE NATIONAL PARK

At a maximum depth of 1,943 feet, this volcanic crater is one of the deepest lakes in the world. Let its clarity and shocking blue color take your breath away.

GASP!

adventures.

While standing on the edge of Crater Lake is one of the most peaceful activities you can do in nature, the lake's history is anything but tranquil—the crater was created by the eruption of Mt. Mazama 7,700 years ago. Yes, this lake was once an active volcano. But when the mountain blew its top, spewing lava and ash into the sky, and then imploded, the explosion left behind what scientists call a **caldera**.

This caldera gradually filled with snow and rainwater and—voilà—the sparkling blue majesty of Crater Lake was born. Because there are no rivers or tributaries flowing into the lake, the water remains pristine. In other words, it's really, really clean. The lake is basically a giant sapphire-blue puddle

📷 *Main image: Wizard Island. Snapshots top to bottom: Phantom Ship island; view from the cliffs.*

THINGS to SEE

. . . one that you're encouraged to splash in.

Mazama Newts: These rough-skinned amphibians were once the top predator in Crater Lake, until non-native crayfish invaded the scene. Now, the newt population is dwindling.

Clark's Nutcrackers: These birds eat the seeds of the whitebark pine tree. They hide seeds to eat later. Any seeds that they don't retrieve develop into new whitebark trees.

THINGS to DO

Boat Cruising: A cruise around the impressive blue waters is unforgettable. As an added bonus, tours include a ranger's talk describing the area's fascinating natural history.

Ski or Snowshoe: If you visit in winter, you'll discover a snowy wonderland. Plenty of trails promise cross-country skiing and snowshoeing.

Park *in* Numbers

51.6
Area covered (sq miles)

125+
Miles of hiking trails

41
Species of mammals

15

OH

CUYAHOGA VALLEY NATIONAL PARK

Bustling with furry creatures, blooming greenery, and burbling creeks, Ohio's only national park is very ecologically diverse. The park is a natural sanctuary where city dwellers can dive into nature—and where anyone can become an explorer.

C uyahoga Valley National Park is an outdoor kingdom of hiking, biking, and horse-riding trails. Here, smack between two Ohio cities, the Appalachian Plateau and the Central Lowlands collide in the valley to create an ecosystem filled with wildlife. About two hundred and fifty species of birds flit through the sky. In the forests and wetlands below, more than 900 plant species provide cover for all kinds of mammals, amphibians, and reptiles. The river that runs through it carries 43 species of fish.

The original occupants, Paleo-Indians, were gone from the valley in the early 1600s, but they were slowly replaced by trappers, mountain men, and other native tribes. As the cities around Cuyahoga Valley grew, so did the park's natural enemy: development. Railroads were built and roads were laid. When Cuyahoga River joined the NPS in 1974, development was stopped in its tracks. Now, the railroad is just another piece of this peculiar park, which is filled with oddities and adventures.

Because the park is so close to big cities, it's easy to take an afternoon jaunt in Cuyahoga Valley. If you only have a few hours to connect with nature, visit one of the park's waterfalls. Brandywine Falls is a stunning 60-foot drop to the river below.

THINGS to SEE

Bald Eagles: This famous bird has returned to the park in fleets, seeking fish. In the fall, watch them performing thrilling midair mating displays, more entertaining than any circus.

Wandering Glider Dragonflies: Ohio's wetlands host 157 species of dragonflies, including the wandering glider. Its iridescent wings will bewitch you.

THINGS to DO

Winter Sports: When snow falls, the valley is a paradise for skiers, snowshoers, and sled heads. All 125 miles of the park's trails are skiable.

Ride the Rails: Trains have been puffing through Cuyahoga since 1880. Hail the train by waving your arms in the air. As far as national parks go, it's a unique ride!

📷 Main image: Blue Hen Falls.
Snapshots from top to bottom:
Bridge over the Cuyahoga River;
the Everett Covered Bridge;
a Canada goose.

REFRESHING.

Park *in* Numbers

5,347
Area covered (sq miles)

134°F
Highest temperature ever
recorded

-282
Lowest elevation
(ft below sea level)

16

CA

DEATH VALLEY NATIONAL PARK

Sand dunes loom on the horizon. The air shimmers with heat. The earth is cracked in odd shapes, like a giant, sand-colored jigsaw puzzle. Ghosts roam in the distance. But squint— you'll see that those are no spirits, they're merely people swathed in white clothing, desperately trying to stay cool.

FORGET HOLLYWOOD— DEATH VALLEY IS CALIFORNIA'S HOTTEST ATTRACTION.

With a record high temperature of 134°F, get ready to experience what it's like to live inside an oven. We recommend driving between the park's geological oddities, such as the sand dunes at Mesquite Flat and the rare aquifer at Salt Creek. Rocks carved by wind smear the landscape with the colors of a half-eaten rainbow Popsicle: reds, mauves, electric greens, and marine blues.

Despite its name—given by Gold Rush miners who almost expired in the heat—the valley is surprisingly full of life. If you're able to, approach a prickly pear cactus (but don't touch!). Try peeping at a desert tortoise emerging from its burrow. Maybe you'll even spot a desert bighorn sheep grazing on a ridge. If you're lucky, you'll visit when spring wildflowers open their colorful petals after winter and spring rains soak the ground. Even the thorny plant life, such as the California barrel cactus, blooms yellow and orange come spring.

Make no mistake—life here is fragile. Survival depends on water, Earth's most precious resource. It hides in springs or seeps.

CALIFORNIA DREAMING, BABY.

📷 *Main images: Zabriskie Point (below); Telescope Peak (opposite). Snapshots from top: male bighorn sheep; wild burros; desert gold flowers.*

THINGS to SEE

Salt Creek Pupfish: These tiny, playful fish can survive the extreme temperatures of Salt Creek.

Wild Burros: Many travelers and miners left things behind in their rush to flee the valley—including a pack of burros, or donkeys. Their braying descendants roam the park today.

THINGS to DO

Ghost Towns: Spots like Rhyolite retain the spirit of the Wild West better than any time capsule.

Join the Jedi: Death Valley is so alien that some of the Star Wars movies were filmed here! Visit the movie set locations, including the Mesquite Flat—Tatooine. Are these the dunes you're looking for?

Park *in* Numbers

9,492
Area covered (sq miles)

172
Species of birds

39
Species of mammals

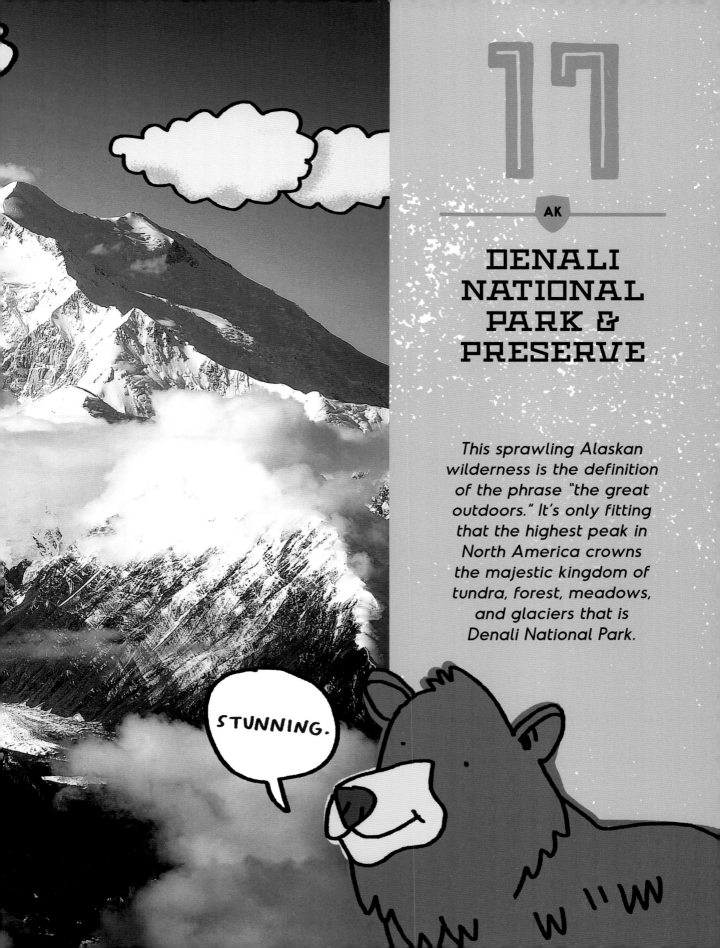

17

AK

DENALI NATIONAL PARK & PRESERVE

This sprawling Alaskan wilderness is the definition of the phrase "the great outdoors." It's only fitting that the highest peak in North America crowns the majestic kingdom of tundra, forest, meadows, and glaciers that is Denali National Park.

STUNNING.

SIX MILLION ACRES.

1t's hard to understand just how big six million acres is—but we'll try to explain anyway. It's bigger than your local park. It's bigger than your whole city. At six million acres, Denali is roughly the size of the entirety of New Hampshire. Here, you'll discover nature for what it really is: raw, fierce, and wildly beautiful.

THINGS to SEE

Wolves: About 100 wolves roam this vast park. Denali is one of the best spots in Alaska (and the world) to spot these ferocious predators in the wild—Denali Park Road is known for sightings. Check out the visitor center to feel a real wolf pelt.

Moose: The second-largest mammal in North America, these elephantine, antlered beasts embody the bigness of Alaska itself as they lumber through the woods. Keep an eye out for them in forested areas by marshes and lakes.

THINGS to DO

Hike It or Bike It: While there are patches of wilderness meant for experienced hikers only, there are many kid-friendly hiking paths and bike loops, too! We recommend the family-friendly Savage River Loop.

Sled Dogs: Don't miss a trip to the kennels. These brave dogs patrol the park in wintertime, helping transport researchers, haul supplies, and keep visitors safe. Arrive early to pet their specially adapted fur! Their coarse outer hair repels water; the underside is extra thick for warmth.

Hovering above it all like a queen on her throne is the 20,310-foot Mt. McKinley—at least it used to be Mt. McKinley. The official name was changed in 2016 to its traditional moniker, Denali, which means "The Great One" in native Koyukon. On a clear day, you can see the glacier-capped summit from almost anywhere in the park. It's a sight that represents the true power of nature—one not easily found in even the most rugged and wild parts of the continental United States. Everything is just bigger in Alaska, including the adventures you'll have when you visit. Take a few hours to drive up Denali Park Road, where you're almost guaranteed to see moose, foxes, caribou, or even grizzlies along its 92-mile stretch.

In the realm of Queen Denali, nature unfolds each spring. Grizzly bears emerge from a long winter's hibernation, claws ready to pluck salmon from white-tipped streams. Caribou and moose shed their winter coats as their fawns wobble on new legs. Wildflowers bloom, decorating the **tundra** as brightly as light bulbs. Through it all, wide-eyed visitors from across the world explore the wilderness of Earth as it once was.

Park *in* Numbers

100
Area covered (sq miles)

100,000
Numbers of sooty terns that
arrive from April to November

16
Bricks used to build Ft. Jefferson
(millions)

18

DRY TORTUGAS NATIONAL PARK

Avast, matey! Come one, come all to this archipelago, a string of islands off the Florida coast guarded by an epic 19th–century fortress.

You wouldn't expect one of the largest brick buildings in the world to dominate a remote tropical island but . . . surprise! In Dry Tortugas, which is only a harrowing boat ride or brief, bumpy flight from Florida's Key West, you'll find an unfinished man-made behemoth: Ft. Jefferson.

Dry Tortugas has served in many strange capacities. The colossal coastal fortress was built to protect access to the Gulf Coast, for trading, and even for use as a prison during the Civil War. Now, instead of waging war, people visit the islands to snorkel, scuba dive, and kayak around the coral reefs. On Dry Tortugas, you can snorkel around shipwrecks and see the sea life on the sunken vessels. Or you can take things slowly like the numerous loggerhead turtles that crowd the beaches.

THINGS to SEE

Magnificent Frigatebirds: These sharp-winged birds are common in the park. Pay attention, and you might see one catch a flying fish in its beak . . . in midair.

THINGS to DO

Snorkeling: Even the shallow waters here host a parade of tropical fish, goliath groupers, lobsters, squid, and octopus. Gear up!

📷 *Main images: Ft. Jefferson and moat in Garden Key (top left); cannon from the Civil War (below). Snapshots, left to right: Crab; lower archways of Ft. Jefferson.*

Park *in* Numbers

2,344
Area covered (sq miles)

15
Maximum size for an adult male
American alligator (ft)

60
Average yearly rainfall (in)

19

FL

EVERGLADES NATIONAL PARK

If you could visit the age of the dinosaurs, would you? What if you didn't have to invent a time machine to spy on the habitat of those long-gone beasts? Imagine this...

There are no roads in sight. Instead, the world is a blanket of swaying saw grass stretching as far as the eye can see. A hot-pink bird plunges its long beak into the murky water and yanks out a wriggling fish. Ginormous plants—some as tall as you—ripple gently in the humid breeze. You notice a log in the marsh below, and then the log moves! Serpentine-yellow eyes rise up to glare at you, followed by an armor-like jaw filled with jagged, sharp teeth.

Don't run! It's only a seven-foot gator raising its head to glance at you before sinking back into the mud. This is Everglades National Park in its swampy, sticky, scaly glory. A unique biozone called a wetland, the Everglades is the largest subtropical wilderness in the United States. It's an intricate maze of marshes, ponds, creeks, and forest, and it's all teeming with life.

There's history hiding among the green, too. Look for shell mounds left behind by the indigenous peoples who traveled these swamps for more than 10,000 years. Over the centuries, the Everglades have been a refuge for Native American tribes and escaped enslaved peoples, who retreated into the swamp to flee war and European colonizers, creating diverse communities united in seeking freedom.

📷 *Main images: Anhinga Trail boardwalk (bottom left); an alligator sunbathes on a fallen tree (above). Snapshots clockwise from top: An Everglades wetland; the Florida butterfly orchid; a stand of flamingos.*

THINGS to SEE

Gators: You're almost guaranteed to see the kings of the Everglades during your visit. They're practically *everywhere*— but they remain so still that they blend in with logs, so be patient!

Florida Butterfly Orchid: Gardening might not be your thing, but trust us: this stunning, unique flower has captivated artists, poets, and photographers throughout history.

THINGS to DO

Kayak: Kayaking here will make you feel like an adventurer exploring a lost jungle. Paddle through tunnels of spooky, gnarled mangroves—and watch out for gators.

Slog: This is a fancy word for walking through the mud. It's a wonderfully messy way to experience nature. Plus, it's educational, so your parents can't say "no." Get dirty for science!

Park *in* Numbers

13,238
Area covered (sq miles)

6
Wild rivers

145
Species of birds

20

AK

GATES OF THE ARCTIC NATIONAL PARK & PRESERVE

Everyone has wished for endless summer days, and here, at the northern edge of the planet, the dream comes true. For a month, the sun never sets, making this ecosystem feel like it exists outside of time itself. The white-dipped horizon stares back at you, like a blank page begging for a story.

no offense, but you probably don't really know nature; it's just a fact of the modern world. Wherever you travel, whether you're on a backyard hike or an epic camping trip in the Rocky Mountains, the human footprint is everywhere. A plane in the sky. A candy wrapper blowing across the ground. The ping of a cell phone. Trying to escape civilization is like trying to get away from your mom or dad when they want you to clean your room. Impossible.

Except we don't believe in *impossible*. Because above the Arctic Circle, where the winds howl and the caribou thunder across frozen plains, true wilderness still exists, waiting for those who dare to face it. This national park might be the most primitive stretch of land on the entire continent. Instead of roads, there are rivers: Alatna, John, Kobuk, Noatak, North Fork of the Koyukuk, and Tinayguk. These freezing waters give you a front-row seat to the best show of all: nature in its purest form. Let the views of glacier-carved valleys sweep you away. The massive 8.4-million-acre wilderness tucked inside the Gates of the Arctic has thousands of

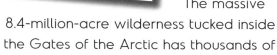

archaeological sites. Each preserves the seminomadic traditions of the indigenous lñupiat and Athabascan peoples. To this day, the descendants of those populations live, hunt, and survive here, in 11 permanent residential communities within the park's boundaries.

When you stand on this ground and survey the larger-than-life skies, it feels as though the modern world has simply disappeared. Gazing toward the northern horizon, you'll expect to meet an ancient god instead of your fellow human.

📷 *Main images: Sukakpak Mountain (top left); wolf tracks in the Brooks Range (below). Snapshot: A snowy owl.*

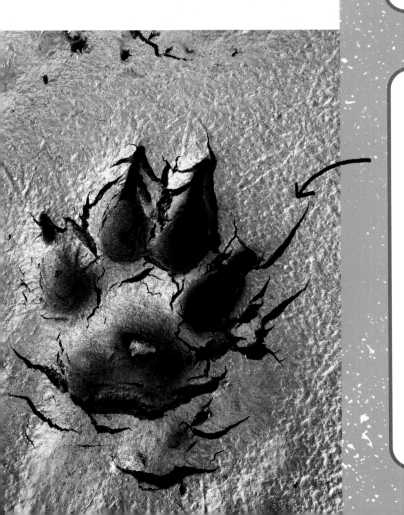

THINGS to SEE

Summer: At the end of the earth, summers are brief—but the sun literally never sets. It's a 24-hour party of migrating birds, dappled fish, caribou, musk oxen, and hungry grizzlies. There's no "lights out" here!

Musk Oxen: These shaggy beasts look like they stepped right out of an ice age. They strut their stuff along the tundra—their personal fashion runway—with their luxurious, long hair swinging in the icy wind. Work it!

THINGS to DO

Become an Archaeologist: There's so much prehistory hiding in the ice, scientists are still uncovering archaeological sites like abandoned camps, mining cabins, and animal remains throughout the park.

Go Birding: From June to August, you can spot ospreys, eagles, yellow-rumped warblers, and snowy owls flitting through the skies alongside sparrows, longspurs, finches, grouse, and the famous arctic tern.

Park in Numbers

0.14
Area covered (sq miles)

630
Height of the Arch (ft)

1,620,000
Number of annual visitors

21

MO

GATEWAY ARCH NATIONAL PARK

Covering about 91 acres, this national park is very small compared to the others. But what it lacks in surface area, it makes up for in height.

At 630 feet tall, the Gateway Arch is more than twice as tall as the Statue of Liberty. The structure was built to commemorate an important moment in U.S. history: westward expansion. Lewis and Clark, the explorers who led the first military exploration of the western frontier, began their trek only steps away from where the giant curve of stainless steel now stands.

Look up—can you see the massive monument swaying in the wind? Don't worry. It was designed to flex and move in the event of high winds.

THINGS to SEE

Museum at the Gateway Arch: This museum provides information about the role St. Louis played in U.S. history, from the time the city was founded until the Arch was built. The coolest part? It's underground!

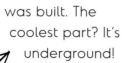

THINGS to DO

Old Courthouse Museum: In 1857, one of the country's most shameful court cases occurred here. Dred Scott, an enslaved man, was denied the chance to sue for his freedom. Now, visitors can learn about slavery and the fight for emancipation.

St. Louis Gateway Arch

ICONIC ANIMALS IN THE PARKS

AMERICAN BISON

The American bison is the national animal of the United States and its largest land animal. Sadly, the country's plentiful herds were nearly hunted to extinction by European colonizers. Thanks to conservation work done with Native American partner organizations, our shaggy friends are making a comeback, with a population of 10,000 and counting!

FACT file

Found In: Badlands, Grand Teton, Theodore Roosevelt, and more
Size: Up to 6 feet tall and 900 pounds
Habitat: Grasslands and savannas
Diet: Herbivore (grasses, lichens)

BALD EAGLE

This iconic bird became the national symbol of the United States in 1782. The bald eagle has a comeback story worthy of a national hero: it nearly went extinct in the 1970s but is now flourishing thanks to conservation efforts. While the majestic, water-loving raptor prefers fish, it will steal food from other predators. Mating pairs often build nests where they flew for the first time.

FACT file

Found In: Parks across the United States, including Acadia, Wrangell-St. Elias, and New River Gorge
Size: Varied depending on habitat, with wingspans up to 8 feet
Habitat: Mainly forests near large bodies of water such as lakes, rivers, and marshes
Diet: Carnivorous (prefer fish but eat small mammals, seabirds, and more)

CALIFORNIA CONDORS

After almost going extinct due to wide-scale lead poisoning and habitat destruction, condors are becoming another conservation success story. The largest bird in North America is recognizable because of its size, bald head, and dark black feathers. Consider yourself lucky if you spot one!

FACT file

Found In: Pinnacles, Grand Canyon, Sequoia and Kings, Zion
Size: 9.5 feet wingspan (average)
Habitat: Varied, including forest, rocky shrubland, grasslands, mountains
Diet: Scavenger carnivore—anything dead

GRAY WOLF

The successful reintroduction of gray wolves into Yellowstone brought balance to an ecosystem in peril by reducing the number of grazing deer and elk. This allowed trees to flourish, stabilizing riverbanks. Beavers and songbirds returned. Scientists are still studying the positive effects of the wolf boom in the park. Spoiler alert: it's a happy ending.

FACT *file*

Found In: Yellowstone, Denali, and more
Size: 30 inches high, up to 6 feet long
Habitat: Varied, including forests, mountains, tundra, grasslands
Diet: Carnivorous (elk, deer)

SALAMANDERS

Hundreds of salamander species thrive within the parks. Salamanders, like all amphibians, split their life between water and land. Scientists call them "indicators" because they indicate environmental danger. Their sensitivity to change makes them an alarm system for ecosystem health. Fascinating species include black-chinned red salamanders and western tiger salamanders, which can glow!

FACT *file*

Found In: Nearly every national park—even in Alaska
Size: 4-6 inches (average), though the hellbender can grow up to two feet
Habitat: In or near fresh water
Diet: Carnivorous (primarily insects)

ENDEMIC SPECIES SPOTLIGHT

Endemic refers to a species that exists in an isolated area and nowhere else in the world. Here are two incredible animals that make the national parks even more unique.

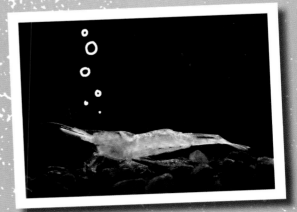

Kentucky Cave Shrimp, Mammoth Cave
This nearly invisible crustacean spends its life within cave streams. It lacks eyes and uses antennules to taste, smell, and touch.

Devils Hole Pupfish, Death Valley
This is the rarest fish in the world. The entire population—175 at last count—lives in a shallow pool near the opening of a deep, watery cavern.

Park *in* Numbers

1,583
Area covered (sq miles)

6,646
Height of Logan Pass (ft)

1,500
Mountain goats

22

MT

GLACIER NATIONAL PARK

Step into Glacier National Park, where you'll discover royal-blue lakes, mountains capped with lush green forests, and glaciers that shine like diamonds—a land fit for queens and kings. No wonder it's called the Crown of the Continent!

Driving in Glacier National Park might feel ordinary at first. Pine forests and lakes blend into a pretty blue-green blur outside your car window. Then, like an eagle soaring in the sky, you turn a bend and suddenly you're 1,000 feet above the valley floor, surrounded by prehistoric granite peaks. Whoa.

There's just something about this park that will make your stomach swoop. Even the main road has a majestic, mysterious name: Going-to-the-Sun Road. It's named after Going-to-the-Sun Mountain, which the local Blackfeet Indians consider a sacred place. Some even say that if you view it from the west, you can spot a face in the snow-covered mountain. Do you see it?

Glacier will feed your love of nature in more ways than one. The park is considered the headwaters for three major North American watersheds. What does that mean? Well, if a snowball melts at the top of a mountain peak and flows into one of Glacier's many rivers and streams, the water could possibly travel all the way to the Pacific or Atlantic Oceans—or both. The snow and ice that melt at Glacier supply the entire country with water. When the snow melts, the hibernating creatures come out to play. Marmots scurry across rocky playgrounds, moose graze on mountain slopes, and grizzlies forage for huckleberries in newly green meadows.

Glacier National Park is home to more than just wildlife—there's plenty of history

THINGS to SEE

Mountain Goats: On a hike, you might run into the park's official mascot: the fluffy white mountain goat. Don't try to follow them! These expert climbers prefer scaling cliffs over taking the easy route.

Canadian Lynx: You might mistake this silvery-brown lynx for a large house cat—if you can spot it at all. This feisty, pointy-eared feline prefers to hunt under the cover of night. That's what we like to call ca-*meow*-flage!

THINGS to DO

Drive Going-to-the-Sun Road: Our professional opinion is that you *don't* drive into the sun— ouch! But cruising along this scenic road is just as electrifying.

See a Glacier: Of the 80 glimmering glaciers that stood tall here in 1850, only 26 are left today. Many experts think that these ice giants will soon melt, too. Go while you still can!

and culture, too. The 1.5-million-acre Blackfeet Indian Reservation is located on the park's eastern border, where 8,600 members of the Blackfeet Nation reside. In 1932, Glacier joined with Waterton Lakes National Park across the border in Alberta, Canada, to create the world's first International Peace Park. Almost 100 years later, the ice-crusted peaks are still a symbol of the friendship between the U.S. and Canada. If you have time, you can even hike or take a boat ride across the border to visit our neighbors to the north!

📷 *Main images: Sunrise at St. Mary Lake (top left); mountain goat (near left). Snapshot: Canadian lynx.*

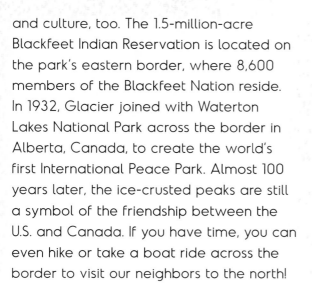

Park *in* Numbers

5,220
Area covered (sq miles)

11
Tidal glaciers

40
Weight of a humpback
whale (tons)

23

AK

GLACIER BAY NATIONAL PARK & PRESERVE

Stacked with massive snowballs called glaciers, this bay is home to one of the most powerful forces on Earth: ice.

GLACIER BAY IS AN ICEBERG FACTORY.

*H*ere, you'll find 11 tidewater glaciers on an unstoppable mission. These frozen giants flow down the mountains, eventually breaking off into the sea in huge chunks. Though the 3,300,000-million-acre park contains all types of terrain, from mountains to temperate rainforest to inlets called fjords, glaciers are what set this park apart from the pack.

Glacier Bay is *on the move*. When an explorer named Captain George Vancouver sailed through here in 1795, all he found was a mountain of ice. Less than a hundred years later, another visiting explorer discovered that the ice had traveled 40 miles. That might not seem like very far—most glaciers move at speeds of a few feet each day—but you only need to glimpse its carved valleys and grooves to understand the power of ice.

Like much of Alaska, Glacier Bay is wild. No roads enter the park. Instead, visitors experience the park by boat. From your vessel, you'll see numerous whales and harbor seals playing in the frigid waters. You might spot a bear or moose swimming across the bay in search of food. Tune in to the epic soundtrack, too: the earsplitting roar of calving icebergs, mingling with the melody of migrating humpback whales. Glacier Bay is a symphony of life and nature, destruction and creation.

📷 *Main image: Breaching humpback whale. Snapshots top to bottom: Aerial view of Glacier Bay; sea otter.*

THINGS to SEE

Sea Otters: These adorable creatures are as mischievous and clever as storybook fairies—if fairies were coated with a thick layer of blubber.

Humpback Whales: After fasting the entire winter in places like Hawai'i or Mexico, around 200 humpback whales hunt in these waters. Their eerie songs are the stuff of legends.

THINGS to DO

By Land: The only developed section of the park is Bartlett Cove, where you can kayak in the bay and touch the massive skeleton of a humpback whale named Snow.

Huna Tribal House: Xunaa Shuká Hít is a permanent clan house where tribal members can connect with their culture while visitors learn about Huna Tlingit history.

Park in Numbers

1,904
Area covered (sq miles)

8,803
Highest point: Pt. Imperial (ft)

1.8
Age of oldest rocks in the canyon (billions of years)

24

AZ

GRAND CANYON NATIONAL PARK

Arguably the most famous national park, you've likely heard of this humongous split in the earth. We're here to tell you that the Grand Canyon is all that it's made out to be. The desert paradise of cliffs, mesas, and sandstone lives up to the hype.

PRACTICALLY EVERYONE KNOWS ABOUT THE GRAND CANYON.

In fact, you can probably picture it in your head. Close your eyes—can you see the red-and-gold cliffs glinting in the blazing sun? Do its flat-topped mesas drip with dramatic shadows, where any number of scaly reptilian desert dwellers await their next meal? Even if you have the wildest imagination in the world, we promise you that the real thing is so much better than anything you can dream up.

📷 Main image: Grand Canyon at sunrise. Snapshots clockwise from top: California condor; the Milky Way over the watchtower; Havasu Falls.

THINGS to SEE

Bats, Bats, Bats: There are more bat species here than almost anywhere else in the United States. One, the little brown bat, chows down on 1,200 mosquitoes per hour.

California Condors: These bald, black vultures—the largest land birds in North America—look like they escaped from a haunted house. There are fewer than 600 individual birds living today.

Prickly Pear Cacti: These cacti show their own colors as if they're trying to rival the sunset: pink, orange, or yellow flowers bloom among the needles, along with fat purple fruits.

THINGS to DO

The Sunset: Fighting the crowds to watch the golden sun splash red, purple, and violet over the canyon walls is worth it. This is nature's most awesome canvas.

Mule Rides: Hopping on the back of a sturdy mule makes for an adventurous and authentic journey to the canyon bottom. If you're up for a bumpy ride, well, giddyup!

Walk the Trail of Time: If you're still sore from the mule ride, slow down by strolling along this path, which offers a self-guided tour of the Grand Canyon's geological timeline.

The Grand Canyon is one of the most magnificent wonders on the planet. Period. No scent comes close to the wafts of piñon trees and sagebrush that perfume the air. At a mile deep, 18 miles wide, and 277 miles long, the canyon's sheer size is hard to appreciate until you've seen it yourself. Even if you know the facts, nothing can measure up to hiking the narrow trails down, down, down to the jade waters of the Colorado River. With millions of years of patience, that wet powerhouse helped create a one-of-a-kind geological marvel.

Here, the rock **strata** tell an ancient story of creation. One lower layer, the Vishnu Schist—also called Vishnu Basement Rocks—is thought to be nearly two billion years old.

For visiting purposes, the canyon is split into two rims: North and South. While it might all seem like a plain old desert at first glance, the park consists of several different ecosystems and a wide range of biological diversity. Plus, the temperature changes as you descend into the canyon. Now that's a trip.

LA LA LA!

📷 Main image: Horseshoe Bend. Snapshots clockwise from top: Cliffs in morning light; Phantom Ranch; sunrise over the Grand Canyon; a dark-eyed junco singing.

Park in Numbers

485
Area covered (sq miles)

13,775
Highest point:
Grand Teton (ft)

173
Average snowfall (in)

WY

GRAND TETON NATIONAL PARK

This mountain-studded treasure chest of natural wonders is waiting to be discovered. With lakes the color of emeralds and creatures around every corner, the Teton Range is a mythical world hiding in plain sight. So strap on some binoculars, pack your map, lace up your hiking boots, and prepare to get dirty— because this park was made for exploring.

If you've ever felt overshadowed by a sibling, you might really get Grand Teton—this stunning, rugged place is often overlooked for its more famous relative, Yellowstone National Park. Of Yellowstone's average four million visitors, nearly one million of those don't make the 10-minute drive to Grand Teton. We're here to let you in on a secret: the quick trip is worth it.

📷 *Main images left to right: Hidden Falls; barn and snow-covered mountains; pronghorn. Snapshots from top: Lupine flowers under a stormy sky; wild horses grazing.*

Unlike your favorite fast-food restaurant, you can't just drive through Grand Teton. Its peaks, valleys, and countless forested nooks beg to be explored. Take Jackson and Jenny Lakes, for example, both of whose shores hide secret waterfalls. The Snake River, dotted with kayaks, rafts, and boats, winds through the forest. The most breathtaking sight in Grand Teton National Park is the Teton Range, which towers over everything! Like a watchful beast, the mountains slumber in the center of the park, daring climbers to scale their snowy peaks. Atop the majestic summits, there is snow most of the year.

Grand Teton is a land of opposites—peaceful valleys humming with birdsong erupt into white-peaked mountains that scrape the sky. That's why spending a day in this park feels like traveling through a portal to different worlds. You can hike through pine-scented forests, have lunch on the banks of a raging river, then spend the afternoon swimming in a glacier-created mountain lake, and top it all off with a tranquil nap in a golden meadow. No matter where you go, you'll be surrounded by as much wildlife as a character in an animated Disney movie: graceful pronghorns and adorable deer nibble the valley sagebrush, while curious otters and bulky elk sip the refreshing river waters. Keep an eye out for fuzzy pika scampering along the craggy terrain! (No, not the kind of pika you train.) These round-eared rascals . . . do they look more like rodents or rabbits?

So, what will your Grand Teton adventure be? *Pika-choose!*

THINGS to SEE

Pronghorns: Called the American antelope, these antlered creatures are actually more closely related to giraffes and okapi. Touring Grand Teton is like embarking on a safari in the United States!

Huckleberry Bushes: Bears can't get enough of these plump, dark berries—they're delicious! When the fruit ripens, the twisty, spindly bushes are downright fairy-tale-esque.

THINGS to DO

Rock Climbing: Like we said, Teton is meant for adventures! To get hands-on—literally—take a ropes and climbing class with a local guide. Don't let the adults talk you out of this one.

Cruise on Jenny Lake: In summer, boats put-put-put between Jenny Lake Visitor Center and Teewinot Mountian. From there, trek to Hidden Falls, a 100-foot-high cascade of water.

Park in Numbers

120
Area covered (sq miles)

13,063
Height of Wheeler Peak (ft)

4,900
Age of "Prometheus," a bristle-cone pine felled in 1964 (years)

26

NV

GREAT BASIN NATIONAL PARK

Below the star-painted sky in eastern Nevada, you'll discover a kaleidoscope of wildly different ecosystems: ancient trees, winding caves, amazing arches, and even a glacier blend together in this unique national park.

White Pine County sits at a mile above sea level—a mile closer to the sky than the rest of the world spinning far below. Although Great Basin National Park is less than 300 miles from Las Vegas, one of the brightest places in the world, there is little to no light pollution at this altitude. The darkness offers picture-perfect views of the galaxy above. If you were one of the sparkling stars shining down on the pine-covered land, you'd be able to see South Snake Range slithering along the ground. You'd twinkle above Wheeler Peak, Great Basin's tallest mountain, sculpted by ice over thousands of years.

Centuries ago, the Fremont people and, later, Western Shoshone tribes,

among others, hunted under the same constellations that watch over Great Basin today. During the Gold Rush, miners searching for riches flooded the California Trail, which carried them right past the park. In the late 1880s, one of these miners made an awesome—and accidental—discovery when he stumbled into a great marble catacomb. Now named Lehman Caves, this burrow-like chamber slinks through the Snake Range and attracts thousands of visitors every year. Because it's so deep, the cavern stays at a constant temperature during every season—even winter!

📷 *Main images: Wheeler Peak (above); Lehman Caves (right). Snapshots from top: The Milky Way above Great Basin; wild horses.*

THINGS to SEE

Great Basin Bristlecone Pines: One of the oldest organisms ever discovered was a bristlecone pine growing in Great Basin—and it was almost 5,000 years old.

Pygmy Rabbits: North America's smallest rabbits dig their burrows in the Great Basin. These gray, fuzzy mammals weigh less than a pound and can fit in the palm of your hand!

THINGS to DO

Night Adventures: On a summer night, view three planets, the Andromeda galaxy, the Milky Way, and the occasional meteor shower. If there's a full moon, you can take a guided night hike!

Cave Tours: Explore stalactites, stalagmites, helictites, flowstone, cave popcorn, and many other geological formations in Lehman Caves, a sprawling cavern inside the park.

Park in Numbers

233
Area covered (sq miles)

150°F/20°F
High and low dune temperatures

750
Tallest dune (ft)

GREAT SAND DUNES NATIONAL PARK

Encircled by a dramatic, white-tipped mountain range and vast grasslands, 30 square miles of sand dunes ripple in front of your eyes, shimmering like a mirage in the desert heat.

A SEA OF SAND.

That's one way to describe Great Sand Dunes National Park, home to the tallest dunes in North America. Dark shadows spill like oil over the massive mounds, turning the stark landscape into a plate of black-and-white cookies. The largest sand dune shadow can grow to more than 700 feet. Stepping into one is as good as exploring the dark side of the moon.

But if you're afraid of the dark, don't worry. The dunes are a gritty, high-speed playground. You can glide down dunes on plastic saucers, sand sleds, or snowboards. You can build castles in the shade of a sandy monster. This park is home to wonders big and small. Inspect some sand under a magnifying glass to discover its hidden world of shapes and colors: you'll see different rock and mineral types inside one grain, from obsidian to turquoise.

So . . . how much sand is here? Well, has a toddler ever dumped shovelfuls of sand on your lap at the beach? Imagine they did that for thousands of years. For millennia, streams, snowmelt, and flash floods have been carrying sand eroded from the San Juan and Sangre de Cristo Mountains to the valley floor. Then, strong winds waged a tug-of-war over the sand, causing it to pile up. Now, thanks to the forces of nature, you can surf the waves of sand tsunamis!

📷 *Main image: Sunrise at Great Sand Dunes. Snapshots top to bottom: A camouflaged spadefoot toad; the dunes.*

THINGS to SEE

Spadefoot Toads: Camouflage makes these amphibians difficult to spot. Try looking for their dark pupils (similar to a cat's) in the sand . . . if they're not burying themselves in it.

Circus Beetles: These sassy insects appear to stand on their heads when threatened. They then spray a smelly chemical into the air to defend themselves.

THINGS to DO

Dune Sledding and Sandboarding: Plunging headfirst down the dunes on a slice of plastic is the rush of a lifetime!

Tubing on Medano Creek: It's not all sand. When the stream of snowmelt is flowing in May and June, you can bob down the creek on an inner tube.

WE DO GUIDED LLAMA TREKS.

Park in Numbers

816
Area covered (sq miles)

19,000+
Plant and animal species
documented here

97
Preserved historic buildings

28

NC TN

GREAT SMOKY MOUNTAINS NATIONAL PARK

With tens of thousands of wildlife species—and still thousands more waiting to be discovered—no other park in the country is brimming with history and life quite like the mist-slathered peaks of the ancient Appalachians.

The Smoky Mountains. Perhaps you've heard of them? They're only one of America's most famous natural wonders. The 522,427 acres of startling, crisp beauty and its convenient location near East Coast cities make the Great Smoky Mountains the most visited national park in the country. But of the more than 12 million travelers per year, most don't stray far from their cars—and they're missing out. Because even if you take only a few steps away from the road toward the misty mountains, you'll find yourself wandering in your own personal fantasyland.

Ask anyone who's gone to the Smokies, and they'll tell you: there's just something magical about these mountains. If you were an eagle flying high above the ring of wrinkly mountains you would glimpse a sea of lush, hardwood trees, swallowed by a persistent, creamy fog that burns off as the sun rises in purple, pink, and silver on the horizon. Connecting all of the park's streams from end to end would stretch them 2,900 miles long. That's wider than the entire state of Alaska! Experience the enchantment for yourself by hiking the park's trails, enjoying a guided horseback ride, snoozing in its many remote campgrounds with your family and friends, or darting behind its numerous and wondrous waterfalls.

📷 Main image: Layered mist in the mountains. Snapshots from top: Tom Branch Falls; a black bear; Jordan's red-cheeked salamander.

As with the entire country, Native American tribes called the Smokies home long before white colonizers made their way there. The Cherokee people had cultivated land and established permanent towns when President Andrew Jackson signed the Indian Removal Act in 1830 and began to forcibly drive Native Americans from their land. In a tragic moment in our nation's history, they were marched to Oklahoma and Arkansas along what we now call the Trail of Tears. But in spite of incredible odds, hardship, and violence, some tribal members evaded persecution by remaining in hiding in the same mountains you can hike through now. The ancestors of these brave individuals live near the park to this day.

THINGS to SEE

Bleeding Hearts: These pink wildflowers are way less gross than their name suggests. Shaped like a cartoon heart wearing a skirt, they blanket the slopes during springtime.

Lungless Salamanders: You can spot up to 24 varieties of skin-breathing salamanders—if they're not hiding under logs or leaf piles.

Yellow Birches: These common trees are covered in bronze bark that smells like a freshly popped bubble of minty gum. Watch in the fall as the leaves seem to transform into gold.

THINGS to DO

Hands-on Science: The Institute at Tremont is an environmental education center that offers summer camps, school programs, and **naturalist** workshops for kids of all ages.

Waterfall Hopping: Heavy rainfall means plenty of rushing—and sometimes raging—waterfalls. You can actually walk behind Grotto Falls.

Light Show: Synchronous fireflies can coordinate their flashing light patterns, and it's the greatest show on Earth. Plan ahead— mating season only lasts for two weeks each year.

Park in Numbers

135
Area covered (sq miles)

8,751
Highest point:
Guadalupe Peak (ft)

1,000+
Species of plants

29

TX

GUADALUPE MOUNTAINS NATIONAL PARK

In the north of the flat Texan desert, Guadalupe Mountains is the undercover spy of the park system—mysterious and overlooked, yet watching all.

Is it invisible? Is it cursed by a spell that keeps people away? Guadalupe Mountains National Park doesn't get noticed as often as some other parks. But about 200,000 visitors each year jaunt through its treacherous, seemingly barren terrain. This unique park is tucked away in a small pocket of the Southwest. It would be easy to miss this place, if the towering rock face of El Capitan wasn't sticking straight up out of the ground like a lightning rod.

But as with every national park, there's something marvelous hiding in all that land—more than its lush streams, forests, and grottoes. The mountains are one of most well-preserved ancient fossil reefs in the world! Once covered by a vast tropical sea, the reef is a geological sandwich of age-old fossils. It boldly displays ancient marine life such as bryozoans, brachiopods, crinoids, gastropods, and sea sponges. Today, the parade of paleontology finds draws scientists from across the globe.

The Guadalupe Mountains were important for indigenous populations, who hunted woolly mammoths here as the ice age came to an end around 10,000 BCE. We know this because they left pottery, baskets, and rock art behind in several caves. In the late 1800s, the mountains were also an unlikely pit stop on a 2,800-mile-long mail route that once connected St. Louis with San Francisco. *Neither snow nor rain nor . . .* mountains?

COOL!

📷 *Main image: Devil's Hall. Snapshots clockwise from top: Guadalupe Mountains; cypress tree on the river; jackrabbit.*

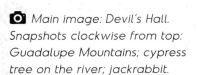

THINGS to SEE

Trilobite Fossils: Trilobites—ancient creatures related to scorpions and spiders—flourished here before dying out in a mass extinction 250 million years ago.

Jackrabbits: You might be familiar with these famously long-eared fuzzballs. But did you know that their oversize ears shed excess heat to help them stay cool in the desert?

THINGS to DO

Festival of Colors: The autumn leaves are particularly bedazzling in the park. Reds, yellows, and oranges shift in the fall breeze at McKittrick Canyon, like a painting come to life.

Wildlife Watching: Head to the numerous springs to scour for creatures like mule deer, coyotes, and hummingbirds. Practice your tracking skills by searching for prints, scat, and burrows.

Park *in* Numbers

47
Area covered (sq miles)

10,023
Highest elevation (ft)

12.8
Size of summit crater (sq mi)

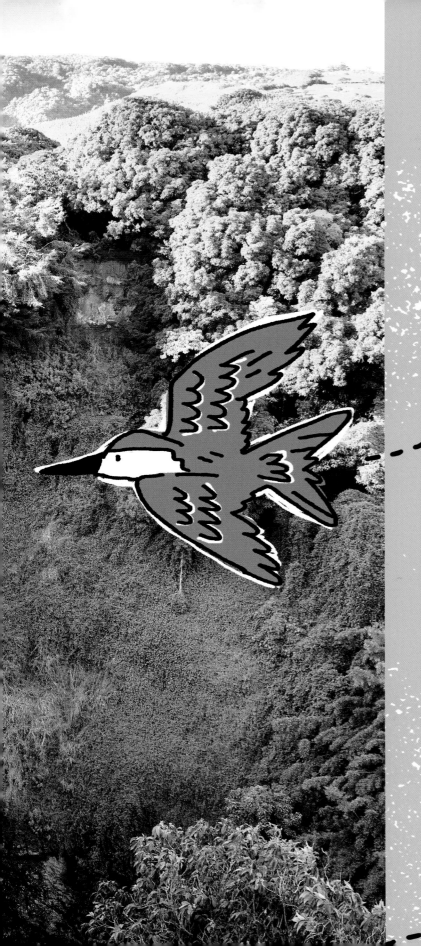

HALEAKALĀ NATIONAL PARK

This ancient volcano—called House of the Sun by Native Hawaiians—rises from the tropical sea, stretching up, up, up into the sky.

S oaring over 10,000 feet, Haleakalā
Volcano is the park's masterpiece.
Standing at the edge of the
volcano's crumbly crater makes you feel like
royalty. The sea-sprayed air fills your lungs,
as you reign over the battlefield of
lava rocks
below.
But amid
a crown of
clouds, the
rising sun
flashes silver
and gold,
claiming its
position as the
one true ruler
of this place.
For this reason,
the summit has
been sacred to
Native Hawaiians for thousands of years. If
you get the chance, read the story of how

the demigod Maui lassoed the sun from this
very peak.

Tourists eager to see the magnificent
sunrise often ignore another side of the
park. Don't be those people! Armed with
your supplies—
sunscreen, water,
insect repellent—
trek along the
jungle road to an
ancient Hawaiian
village site at
the foot of the
lava-breathing
behemoth.
Just like
elsewhere in
the Hawaiian
Islands,
the isolated
location has allowed flora and fauna
to evolve into a bouquet of unique
species. Several rare birds like the Kiwikiu,

'Akohekohe, and Nukupu'u, all species of honeycreepers, were thought to be extinct before they flaunted their curved beaks and lovely songs in the sun- and star-drenched skies.

 Main images: Oheo Gulch (left); Haleakalā Volcano crater (right). Snapshot: Volcanic crater landscape.

THINGS to SEE

Nēnēs: Also known as the Hawaiian goose, these endangered birds build their nests in the volcano's crater. They evolved webbed feet for strutting on the rough terrain of cooled lava flows. Wow!

Haleakalā Silverswords: Oddly enough, these rare plants—which look like hedgehogs—belong in the daisy family. They bloom only once in a lifetime, but they can live up to 90 years.

THINGS to DO

Stargazing: Haleakalā's skies are so dazzling that solar observatories have been constructed here. In the summer, rangers often lead stargazing programs at Hosmer Grove Campground.

Kīpahulu: This rugged coastland has streams that contain gobies and other fish species evolved from ancient saltwater life-forms. Though its natural pools are closed due to rockslides, you can still spy on seals, sea turtles, and whales from the shore.

Park *in* Numbers

554
Area covered (sq miles)

72
Number of Kīlauea Volcano
confirmed eruptions

90
Percent of Kīlauea's surface
covered in lava flows

HAWAI'I VOLCANOES NATIONAL PARK

Life and land here are always buzzing and sizzling and moving, just like the earth that churns deep beneath Hawai'i Volcanoes National Park. It is a kaleidoscope of color smack in the middle of the vast, flat ocean. Pele, the Hawaiian goddess of volcanoes, rules this place.

For over 70 million years (longer than the dinosaurs have been extinct), volcanoes have been sculpting the Hawaiian Islands. Lava cooled into piles of rock, growing taller and taller as they climbed out of the deep blue sea. Now these ancient fire-belching mountains are a paradise for the most unique plant and animal life in the whole world. See? With a little patience and a smidgen of boiling-hot magma, you can do anything!

Today Hawai'i, nicknamed the Big Island, is still an active volcano. Don't worry—Hawaiian volcanoes rarely explode. Instead, the park oozes lava. When these molten rivers flow into the ocean, you can see steam rising up in giant, billowing clouds. Red-hot lava hitting salt water hisses like a hundred snakes.

But it isn't all about lava. The park protects many diverse habitats, including a rainforest, beaches, and even an alpine mountain. And did we mention there's a lava lake? Halema'uma'u Crater holds a pool of churning volcano juice. What else would you expect from the residence of the hot-tempered Hawaiian goddess of volcanoes and fire, Pele?

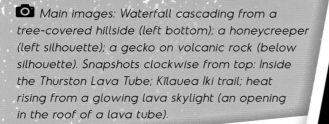
📷 Main images: Waterfall cascading from a tree-covered hillside (left bottom); a honeycreeper (left silhouette); a gecko on volcanic rock (below silhouette). Snapshots clockwise from top: Inside the Thurston Lava Tube; Kīlauea Iki trail; heat rising from a glowing lava skylight (an opening in the roof of a lava tube).

THINGS to SEE

Honu'ea (Hawaiian Hawksbill Turtle): This endangered reptile is born on the park's beaches. Hatchlings face many predators on their dangerous journey into the sea. Go, hatchlings, go!

Bird Species: Our feathered friends dominate the park. From tiny rainbow-colored honeycreepers to the 'Io (Hawaiian hawk), many different kinds of birds call this island home.

THINGS to DO

Caving: When lava erupts, it leaves behind lava tubes, or tunnels. Some are big enough to drive a school bus through! Explore Nāhuku (Thurston Lava Tube).

Appreciate Hawaiian Culture: Don't miss the Volcano Art Center, where hula hālau (schools that teach hula) students dance and hundreds of native artisans share their crafts with visitors.

Park in Numbers

8.7
Area covered (sq miles)

143°F
Average temperature of the hot springs' water

700,000
Gallons of hot water used in bathhouses and for drinking fountains daily

32

AR

HOT SPRINGS NATIONAL PARK

A teeny-tiny marvel, one of America's smallest national parks guards nature's most relaxing bubble baths. People have been soaking in this steamy sanctuary for centuries.

HOW'S THE WATER?

Gazing into the curtain of steam that always hangs over Hot Springs National Park will give you a good idea of what Earth once looked like long ago. The national park is centered around 47 boiling brooks. Each geological Crock-Pot contains warmed water, the likes of which once covered Arkansas in thick vapor. Many people believe that the ancient steam has healing powers.

We know for a fact that the water comes from rainfall, deep-heated during a 4,400-year journey into the earth and back again. The spring has been popular for thousands of years. Caddo, Choctaw, and Cherokee tribes bathed here long before Europeans colonized the land. Native tribes also quarried stone in the area to make tools.

📷 *Main images: Hot-water cascades (above); grassy meadow and trail (right). Snapshots top to bottom: Hot Springs wilderness; mineral hot water.*

THINGS to SEE

Red River Waterdogs: You're barking up the wrong tree if you think these slick amphibians are canines. Like other salamanders, the frilly-gilled mudpuppy can regrow its limbs.

THINGS to DO

Take the Plunge: While you can't go into the outdoor thermal pools (for your safety), the Buckstaff Bathhouse allows children 10 and up to relax in their waters.

Park in Numbers

23.9
Area covered (sq miles)

15
Length of shoreline (miles)

350+
Confirmed
species of birds

33

IN

INDIANA DUNES NATIONAL PARK

At the edge of Lake Michigan, one of the Great Lakes, you can dive into geological history. This landscape of rolling dunes is a picturesque record of the continent's last major glacier.

You don't have to travel to the ocean to enjoy a day at the beach. At Indiana Dunes, you can sunbathe on the sandy shoreline of Lake Michigan, the heart of this national park. One of the five Great Lakes, Lake Michigan is the largest lake in the world that's located in a single country. It provides drinking water to millions of people. See for yourself why it's often called a freshwater sea—the seemingly endless water stretches to the horizon. But don't worry, there be no pirates here!

If you're not feeling seaworthy, use your land legs to hike the 15,000 acres of marsh, bogs, wetlands, and other diverse habitats bursting with flora and fauna. Inland, large dunes—mainly the Glenwood, Tolleston, and Calumet—rise hundreds of feet in the air. These ridges were left behind thousands of years ago as Lake Michigan changed shape. Today, the dunes are covered in blankets of plant life, including grass fields and oak forests.

THINGS to SEE

Wood Frogs: Have you ever wondered what frogs and car engines have in common? Antifreeze! At least in the case of this species, whose body has a superhero-like ability to partially freeze during the winter.

Mount Baldy: At more than 100 feet, this monstrous "living" dune is a giant's sandcastle. Despite its size, Mount Baldy is on the move—it shifts approximately 5 to 10 feet every year.

RIBBIT

THINGS to DO

Shelf Ice. In winter, dangerously low temperatures create floating ice packs across Lake Michigan. These chunks smash into frozen patches along the shore to create magnificent, Arctic-like landscapes of snow and ice along the beach. The view is extraordinary, but remember, it's only for looking. Shelf ice is unstable, dangerous, and must be viewed from a distance.

Bird-watching is especially popular here. Hundreds of songbird and waterfowl species skim the dunes and dip into the waves. If you visit during spring or fall migration, you might see a worm-eating warbler or a piping plover. The park even helps host the annual Indiana Dunes Birding Festival every May!

📷 *Main images: The forest floor in Indiana Dunes (left); a worm-eating warbler (above). Snapshots top to bottom: A Lake Michigan beach; sand dunes.*

Park *in* Numbers

850
Area covered (sq miles)

31
Wolves (in 2023)

2,060
Moose (estimated in 2019)

34

MI

ISLE ROYALE NATIONAL PARK

This park is made up of 400 islands. Isle Royale is the largest, and it is a fortress of spruce, pine, and birch trees in the northern area of Lake Superior.

*I*sle Royale sits in the largest and coldest of the Great Lakes. The remote location makes this 893-square-mile national park one of the country's least visited. Stony and silent, it emerges from the glassy water like a riddle waiting to be solved.

THINGS *to* SEE

Wolves: As of 2023, there are 31 wolves that roam here. That might not seem like a lot, but there are more wolves now than in previous years. Superhero scientists are tracking them carefully to make sure numbers keep going up.

THINGS *to* DO

Tobin Harbor: Exploring by boat is the best way to experience the marine life on Isle Royale. Paddle the calm waters of this harbor in a canoe or a kayak.

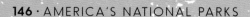

📷 *Main images: Sunrise at Rock Harbor (above); a gray wolf (near right, silhouette); gneiss shoals can be seen underwater surrounding Shaw Island, just outside Isle Royale National Park (far right).*

Life here hasn't always been sparse. In fact, its natural resources have been mined for centuries. First, the Ojibwe people hammered copper out of the bedrock. Later, fishers caught whitefish and lake trout in staggering numbers. Then, workers chopped down towering spruce and balsam trees. When the park was established in 1940, the forests were already growing back. Now, they circle the isle's many freshwater lakes and provide a stately residence for wildlife.

Isle's woods are a stage for the world's oldest performance—the dance between predator and prey. For decades, wolves and moose populations have fought for survival. Like the forest itself, these species are now searching for a second chance.

Park *in* Numbers

1,242.5
Area covered (sq miles)

8,000+
Rock climbing routes

5
Desert fan palm oases

35

CA

JOSHUA
TREE
NATIONAL
PARK

Crooked trees jut out of the ground. Like many tentacled creatures, their spiny arms wave at you, begging you to enter this Southern California desert, a crossroads for wily coyotes and clever roadrunners alike.

WATCH FOR COYOTES.

TEN PACES, COWBOY.

That's as far as you'll need to go before feeling the irresistible tug to enter Joshua Tree National Park. Here, giant boulders look as if they were rolled across the desert floor by humongous dung beetles. In jumbled, uneven piles, the Creamsicle-colored rocks seem to glow in the rays of the desert sun. At night, under a full moon and lightning-bright stars, geological formations resemble ruins from an alien world. The park's bizarrely bent trees only add to the strangeness of the picture. As you peer out at them, you might find yourself trying to unlock an ancient code spelled out by their angular branches. And you may stumble upon another surprise: a real desert oasis shaded by California fan palms. It turns out that the park contains a hidden story, one of tectonic plate action. The park has hundreds of earthquake faults, which created many of its formations.

Joshua Tree functions as a museum, too—a museum of mistakes. You can see historical artifacts from American miners who sought silver and gold but never found it, and homesteaders who abandoned their land when no rain came. But if you travel to Pinto Basin, you'll discover a land

THINGS to SEE

Joshua Trees: The park is named after these 40-foot-high yucca plants, which bloom with white flowers in the spring. But their twisted branches are easy to recognize in any season!

Greater Roadrunners: Roadrunners make up for the lack of bird species found in Joshua Tree. Daredevils that can run faster than humans, these tan cuckoos can kill rattlesnakes.

THINGS to DO

Rock Climbing: There are more than 8,000 climbing routes, for beginners and experts alike! During climbing season, introduce yourself to the park's climbing ranger for some tips and tricks.

Blast to the Past: Joshua Tree was once crawling with homesteaders, miners, and ranchers seeking fortune. Explore Keys Ranch or Silver Bell Mine to experience their rugged life firsthand.

that has been inhabited for over 8,000 years. Native Americans, including the Serrano, Chemehuevi, and Cahuilla tribes, still call this desert home. On any given day, they gather desert plants for food, medicine, and basket weaving, according to their traditions.

Its position at the border of two deserts means that Joshua Tree is home for all kinds of animal and plant life. In the south, the Sonoran Desert carpets the land like a big, sandy lizard-and snake-filled blanket. On a clear day, you can see as far as Mexico. The Colorado Desert, part of the Sonoran Desert, blooms with the red flowers of spiky ocotillo plants. Watch out for cholla cacti, whose spines seem to "jump" out at passersby. Farther north is where you'll find the rare Joshua tree. The finicky plant prefers the milder climate of the Mojave Desert in that area.

📷 *Main images: Joshua Tree National Park (upper left); Joshua tree (above, silhouette). Snapshots clockwise from top: Cholla Cactus Garden; a rock formation in Joshua Tree; a greater roadrunner crossing the road.*

Park *in* Numbers

6,250
Area covered (sq miles)

2,200
Brown bears

9,000
Years of human habitation

36

AK

KATMAI NATIONAL PARK & PRESERVE

Another hidden, remote Alaskan gem, this park is a refuge for brown bears. Behind a curtain of haze, the creatures remain tucked away from the world in a landscape worthy of their might, stature, and grace.

An abundance of animals and a vast and varied landscape. This is real life in Katmai National Park and Preserve. A salmon wriggling between water-slicked claws. A mother bear shaking moisture from her thick fur. Sea lions swimming and red foxes trotting. And we can't forget the volcano smoke rising in the distance. These images make visiting this park feel like stepping into a postcard. It's Alaska, so of course the park is ginormous, and there are many experiences to be had, even some you might not have seen on any postcards.

THINGS to SEE

Sea Lions: Spend some time on the gorgeous coast to observe curious sea lions mingling with entertaining sea otters. The flippered sea lions hang out in massive—and very loud—colonies.

Beavers: Unbothered by human activity, beavers keep busy. Watch as they construct their lodges with native branches from nearby.

THINGS to DO

Bear Watching: This is the reason roughly 35,000 people make the trek to Katmai every year. Try Brooks Falls, where bears snatch leaping salmon in midair. It's better than anything on TV.

Brooks Falls: Bears aside, this simple half-mile hike leads to plenty of spectacular views. Find the viewing platforms on the trail to spot bears submerging themselves in the rushing waters.

If you venture deeper into the park, you'll discover lost lakes, Alaskan Native cultural traditions, and something called the Valley of Ten Thousand Smokes. The name explains quite a bit about the site. The valley is filled with **ash flow**—you know, volcano vomit! For years, the valley was polka-dotted with smoking fumaroles, small openings where hot gas escapes. After being drenched with volcano spew, the land was transformed into the eerily naked landscape you see today. In fact, that's why Katmai was originally founded: scientists wanted to study the valley's active volcanism. As they say, the rest is history!

📷 *Main images: A grizzly bear family in Katmai (left); rugged coastline (above). Snapshots top to bottom: A coastal brown bear; a pair of sea lions.*

Park *in* Numbers

1,047
Area covered (sq miles)

191
Species of birds

400+
Miles of coastline

37

AK

KENAI FJORDS NATIONAL PARK

You might not know what fjords are . . . yet. The images of the long, narrow inlets of dark, mysterious seawater in Kenai will forever remain in your imagination.

📷 *Main images: Resurrection Bay (top left); a puffin (silhouette); Exit Glacier, Harding Icefield (below right). Snapshots clockwise from top: Coastline at sunset; wild seal in Kenai waters; an orca.*

G laciers left their mark on this Alaskan landscape. Deep grooves that were carved in the earth and flooded with water are so magical that they needed a special name: fjords. Tracing them backward leads you to a glimmering block of ice called the Harding Icefield. This is where it all began.

Though the Loch Ness monster is from Scotland, it's easy to conclude that it would be right at home in the depths of Kenai's fjords. Is that a flash of scales? A tail whipping in the rippling deep?

It's probably just the reflection of an elephantine iceberg bobbing in the water. But there is real sea life living out dramas below the waves. Porpoises and whales cruise just under the surface, while sea otters and puffins swim playfully along the icy edge.

WELCOME!

THINGS to SEE

Orcas: There are about 300 orcas gallivanting in the park's waters. Merciless hunters, they're known as "killer whales" for a reason.

THINGS to DO

Sea Kayaking: There's nothing like kayaking through icebergs to a soundtrack of crackling ice.

Park *in* Numbers

721.7
Area covered (sq miles)

8,200
Maximum depth of
Kings Canyon (ft)

267.4
Height of General Grant,
tallest tree (ft)

KINGS CANYON NATIONAL PARK

The Sierra Nevada is a mismatched collage of giant sequoia trees, sharp granite cliffs, and plunging river canyons. There's something for everyone here.

Once called a rival to its neighbor Yosemite (which is a big deal), this all-around stunning national park could give any landmark a run for its money. With sequoias that reach skyward and steep canyon walls that dive low, Kings Canyon literally reaches new heights *and* depths of wonder. But why take our word for it? See the dizzying views for yourself by pausing at stops such as Junction View to peek over the precipice. The roaring white water below will look like nothing but a faraway white smudge.

No matter your vantage point, the park is an excellent place to reconnect with mother nature. Hike into the peaceful, majestic forest. The only soundtrack along the trail is silence itself. Well, maybe there's a *smidgen* of birdsong. If you're looking to get rowdier, Kings Canyon has an array of natural swimming pools and waterfalls to cool off in. If you visit in winter, you can enjoy the park in a pair of snowshoes. Though you might not be ready for an epic backpacking trip like the experienced hikers you're sure to meet on your adventure, many families camp out at the feet of sequoias. Slumbering next to giants is an experience for all ages!

📷 *Main images: Kearsarge Lakes in fall (above); Kings River (below right). Snapshot: A black bear cub.*

THINGS to SEE

Black Bears: Who is the king of Kings Canyon? The black bear, of course. Its scientific name, *Ursus americanus*, sounds fittingly fancy. Remember that they can be black, brown, golden, or even cinnamon colored.

California Spotted Owls: This nocturnal creature is very, very hard to spot. Its ink-black eyes melt into the darkness. If you're camping under the sequoias, listen for their distinctive calls as you fall asleep!

THINGS to DO

Swimming: The summertime swimming holes in Kings Canyon are fit for royalty! Double- and triple-check conditions with a park ranger before diving in.

General Grant Tree Trail: Follow this trail to discover the second-largest tree in the entire world: General Grant, named for the 18th president, Ulysses S. Grant.

Park *in* Numbers

2,734.4
Area covered (sq miles)

402
Plant species

162
Bird species

39

AK

KOBUK VALLEY NATIONAL PARK

Experience ice-cold sand dunes, an army of migrating caribou, and rainbows of flashing salmon in this remote tundra.

$\mathcal{E}$arlier, we tried to paint a picture of how rugged Alaska is. Here, the wilds of Alaska get even wilder. Perched above the Arctic Circle, Kobuk Valley is a remote empire of sand dunes tucked between queenly mountain ranges. Like so many features in Alaska, the dunes were created by glaciers. The dunes are actually gigantic piles of glacial dust produced by the grinding of ice over earth.

THINGS to SEE

Boreal Forest: Also known as taiga or "snow forest," this sprawl of pine trees ends abruptly here, giving way to the vast Arctic tundra.

THINGS to DO

Wildlife Watching: Migrating caribou are the highlight of the park, though grizzlies, mink, loons, moles, lynx, and even wood frogs dot the tundra.

In the fall and spring, hundreds of thousands of caribou cross the Kobuk River in a great migration, one of the few large migrations that still happen. They leave behind deep footprints in the soft dunes, like the camels of Egypt do. But don't try to hop on a caribou's back for a ride across the tundra. These heavy-hoofed beasts are as untamed as the wilderness itself.

Not many people can withstand the park's conditions. Only Alaskan Natives have remained steadfast; they've been harvesting migrating caribou for 9,000 years.

📷 *Main images: Kobuk Valley National Park (top); caribou antlers (middle); caribou migrating across the dunes (bottom). Snapshots left to right: Caribou in summer; Canadian lynx.*

Park in Numbers

6,297
Area covered (sq miles)

0
Roads

147,000+
Red salmon that annually
migrate into Lake Clark

40

AK

LAKE CLARK NATIONAL PARK & PRESERVE

Four million acres. How is it possible that these four million acres of Alaskan wilderness remain largely unknown to lovers of the outdoors.? In true Alaskan fashion, Lake Clark definitely plays it cool.

Coastal bays, glaciers, volcanoes, tundra, freshwater lakes, wildlife . . . the abundance and grandness of Lake Clark National Park and Preserve are extreme, even for Alaska! Not that we're complaining. The absolutely gigantic park has not one but two major mountain ranges. The Neacola and the Chigmit connect here, pressing their massive gray foreheads and snowy white beards together in contemplation.

It's no surprise that glaciers have provided Lake Clark with much of its bounty.

While most of the 24 original ice queens have slipped from the mountains, they left behind lakes and streams brimming with salmon in their wake. Brown bears hungry for the fish descend upon Lake Clark in shuffling herds, resulting in one of the highest brown bear populations in the world.

Part of the reason the park has remained so unspoiled is that it is only accessible by small plane. But it's not an impossible trip! Let the salmon inspire you. It can't be that much harder than swimming upstream, right?

📷 *Main images: Sow grizzly and three cubs walking along the shore of Crescent Lake (above); a pair of puffins (near right); Alaskan brown bear cubs with their mother (far right). Snapshots left to right: Lake Clark from the air; American bald eagle.*

THINGS to SEE

Brown Bears: Can you tell we're very interested in bears? The shaggy, shuffling beasts are utterly captivating, and at Lake Clark you're almost guaranteed to see one.

Cook Inlet: The 123-mile-long coastline is a favorite of—yep— mother bears and their cubs. Share the rocky shore (at a distance) to find the grasslike sedge plant, razor clams, and fish.

THINGS to DO

Fishing: Casting your line into Lake Clark's salmon-filled waters is a unique experience. It's one of the only places in the world where a brown bear might be waiting on the opposite shore, hungrily eyeing your catch.

Kijik Landmark: Park archaeological sites are connected to the inland Dena'ina Athabascan people, who have lived in the Lake Clark area for thousands of years. Kijik roughly translates to "place where people gather" in Dena'ina.

Park *in* Numbers

166.2
Area covered (sq miles)

10,457
Height of Lassen Peak (ft)

1915
Last major eruption (May 22)

41
CA
LASSEN VOLCANIC NATIONAL PARK

Where the Sierra Nevada, Cascade volcanoes, and the Great Basin Desert collide, there's bound to be geologic turbulence. Fasten your seat belts, because we're in for a bumpy ride!

UP TO 500,000 PEOPLE VISIT LASSEN VOLCANIC NATIONAL PARK EACH YEAR.

This volcanically active zone, which first ignited 825,000 years ago, has never quite fizzled out. Here, every single type of volcano can be found: shield, lava dome, cinder cone, and composite. To top it off, Lassen is also populated by boiling mud pots, steaming vents, and acidic hot springs. Some people just can't handle the heat.

Lassen is a trickster. Its landscape is composed of gently rolling, tree-dotted sand hills, known as Painted Dunes. They give the appearance of calm. From a distance, you'll mistake this picturesque pinkish landscape for a watercolor painting. In spring, wildflowers scatter over the alpine peaks. However, there's trouble brewing underneath all that tranquility. You need only visit the **hydrothermal** areas to witness the earth percolating like coffee brewing. It's a repeating playlist of bubble and hiss, bubble and hiss.

Because it's at the crossroads of three major ecosystems—Cascade, Sierra Nevada, and Great Basin—Lassen has long served as a meeting place for Native American tribes. To this day, Maidu, Yana, and Atsugewi peoples hunt there in the summer, in addition to gathering plants used for food and medicine. Tribal members also give talks about their heritage.

📷 *Main image: The Painted Dunes as seen from the top of the Cinder Cone. Snapshots clockwise from top: Vista from Lassen Peak; a tortoiseshell butterfly; Devils Kitchen.*

THINGS to SEE

Whitebark Pines: These conifers often twist themselves into crooked, antler-like shapes. Unfortunately, they're especially vulnerable to climate change.

California Tortoiseshell Butterflies: These orange-brown butterflies can sometimes be seen by the thousands! No one is quite sure why. We're happy to let the butterfly army take flight.

THINGS to DO

Fantastic Lava Beds: The name says it all! The thick, black, bumpy sheet of solidified lava stretches for several miles. It's an absolute must for first-time visitors.

Bumpass Hell Trail: Suggest that your family walk the trail. Despite its misleading (and slightly naughty) name, this easy hike leads to the largest hydrothermal zone.

WHAT DID YOU SAY?!

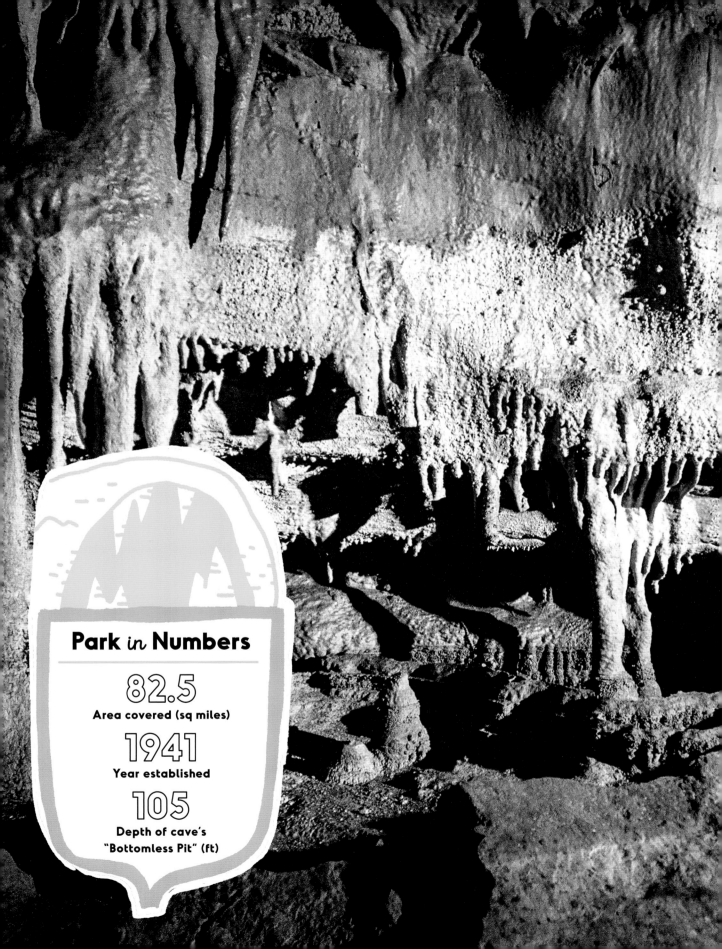

Park *in* Numbers

82.5
Area covered (sq miles)

1941
Year established

105
Depth of cave's
"Bottomless Pit" (ft)

42

MAMMOTH CAVE NATIONAL PARK

Chambers the height of football goalposts. Murky rivers crawling with cave creatures. From cave floor to ceiling, Mammoth encompasses a subterranean realm of oddities.

Mammoth Cave National Park's caverns rise above you like big top circus tents. There are even acrobatic demonstrations from—you guessed it—actual bats. So step right down into Mammoth's festival of wonder and curiosities, which thrives hundreds of feet beneath the ground.

Mammoth doesn't need to pull any death-defying stunts to be special. After all, being the world's longest cave system is pretty impressive. Even more spectacular are the formations, like cave coral, striated "cave bacon," and frozen waterfalls that speckle 420 miles of tunnels. With its natural stores of saltpeter—an ingredient in gunpowder—Mammoth might be the most explosive show on Earth!

HI

📷 *Main images: Historic entrance into the cave (below); interior of the cave (right). Snapshot: Mossy rock overhang in the forest.*

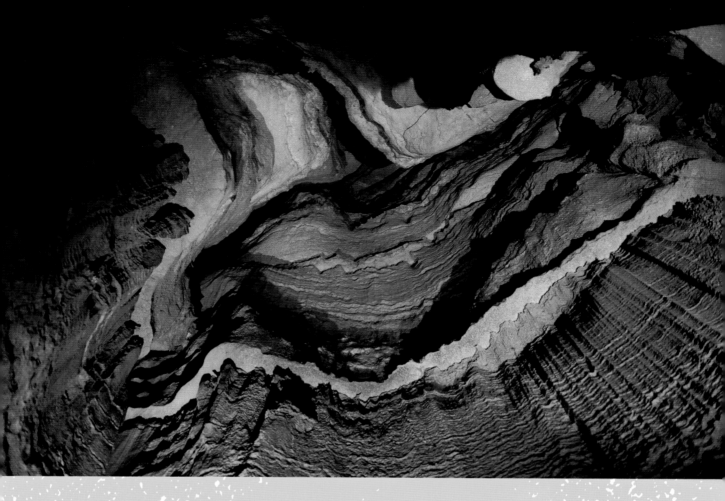

THINGS to SEE

Mammoth Cave Crayfish: This ghostly crustacean needs to hit the beach. Over time, the dark environment of their cave streams made them small and extremely pale. They're shells are nearly see-through.

Boo!

THINGS to DO

Cave Tours: You must participate in a guided tour to experience Mammoth. We love the tour themes: a historical tour will take you to the old tuberculosis ward, while the Violet City lantern tour is conducted by lantern light.

NATIONAL PARKS AT NIGHT

When the sun sets in a national park, the day might be over, but the adventure is just beginning. Night brings a whole new world to explore. Plus—it's the perfect excuse to stay up past your bedtime. For science!

3, 2, 1...LIFTOFF!

Forget the space shuttle, astronauts, because the national parks bring outer space to you. Distance from city lights means parks hold the darkest skies in the country. In fact, Big Bend is thought to be the darkest sky in the contiguous 48 states. Imagine constellations winking through a mighty tree canopy in Sequoia or a comet blazing across the moonless dark in Great Basin. It's like the parks are in a race to see which has the most amazing night skies.

Look up to see constellations that have inspired myths, music, and stories for thousands of years. For a closer look, head to one of the many parks equipped with telescopes and observatories to help visitors understand the stars like never before. The National Park Service doesn't just love their night skies, they fight to preserve them as an endangered natural resource. As of 2023, 17 national parks are protected nighttime environments.

COOL!

NIGHT-TASTIC NATURAL PHENOMENA

Every national park holds nighttime wonders, but some have unique natural phenomena—special things that happen only at night.

The Aurora Borealis: Also known as the Northern Lights, this natural light show is caused by Earth's magnetic field interacting with solar wind. Picture green and purple waves splashed across the dark sky. This occurs close to the Arctic Circle, which means many Alaskan parks set the stage for this dazzling light display. But you might catch the show at Voyageurs or Isle Royale. So do your solar homework! The dance between Earth and sun is not to be missed.

Bioluminescence: Though it is rare, lucky park visitors can spot glow-in-the-dark wildlife. Bioluminescence is created by chemical reactions and serves varied purposes, including mating, communication, and defense. "Foxfire" fungi, like the jack-o'lantern mushroom, emit an eerie green glow. If you're into creepy-crawlies, the *Motyxia* millipede at Sequoia National Park is for you. During the day, the 60-legged creature looks normal; when dark falls, it emits a stunning blue light.

DESERT EXTREMES

The desert is as extreme as it gets—but did you know the arid landscape completely transforms at night? Boiling daytime temperatures plummet when the sun goes down. This happens because sand is not good at trapping heat. Many nocturnal and crepuscular wildlife species have survived in desert ecosystems by taking advantage of this cooldown. Some plants, too, will wait to bloom in lower temperatures. Joshua Tree, Arches, and Death Valley are just a few of the desert-rific parks you can explore in the dark . . . if you become nocturnal, too!

Synchronous Fireflies: You can attend a midnight dance party at Congaree or Great Smoky Mountains National Park! In late spring, large numbers of fireflies participate in a mating display worthy of an alien planet. "Synchronous" means all the insects blink at the same time, creating pulses of light that illuminate the nighttime forest.

📷 *Main images: Milky Way at Balanced Rock, Big Bend National Park (left), Joshua Tree National Park (above), foxfire fungi (top).*

Park in Numbers

81
Area covered (sq miles)

8,572
Height of Park Point (ft)

100+
People who once
lived at Cliff Palace

43

CO

MESA VERDE NATIONAL PARK

In a dry corner of Colorado, an ancient city rises from the dust.

COOL!

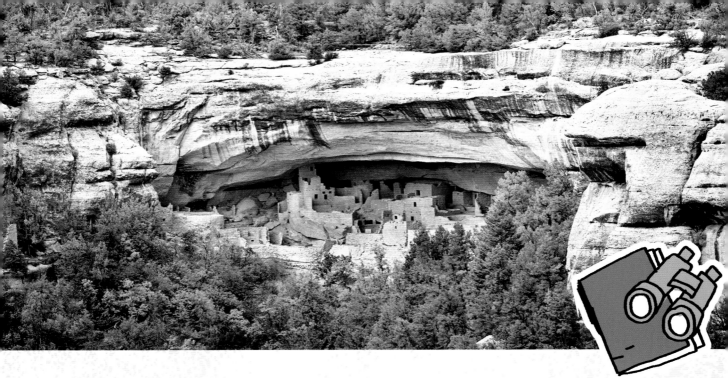

In Mesa Verde, you're gonna get dir-tay! Though its lush green mesas, biodiversity, and wild horses are stunning, the park's natural features alone don't draw visitors. No—people arrive to this park like flocks of migrating birds to experience an astonishing piece of history: the cliff dwellings.

Until 1300 CE, Ancestral Puebloans inhabited this area. In that time, they achieved one of ancient America's most impressive architectural feats: they carved 600 cliff dwellings into sheer rock faces. These alcoves were not by any means crude. Rather, they were a honeycomb of homes, ceremonial centers called "kivas," and storage units. The best part? The dwellings hung hundreds of feet above the valley floor. (And you thought the top bunk was cool.)

At Mesa Verde, getting hands-on is a requirement. To get up close and personal with the dwellings, you must scramble up ladders, scale rock, and crawl through narrow tunnels. Even with helpful railings and rangers, it's still a whole lot of work. But no park is going to scratch your itch for exploration quite like Mesa Verde.

Today, we don't understand why the Ancestral Puebloans abandoned this site. But browsing the rooms for yourself, puzzling over the relics like a detective, is hands down the most exciting way to approach a history lesson.

When you're done being an archaeologist, there are plenty of intriguing sites in the canyons and mesas. No matter where the day takes you, we'll bet that the experience of exploring Mesa Verde will linger in your head long after you leave.

📷 *Main images: Ancient Pueblo cliff dwelling (above); inside a kiva at Mesa Verde National Park (right).*

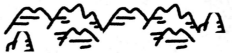

THINGS to SEE

Mexican Spotted Owls: *Whoo? Whoo? Whoo?* These wise owls prefer to linger in old-growth forests, using high canopies to nest well above the hubbub below. Their night-black eyes make them easy to spot.

THINGS to DO

Balcony House: On the obstacle course of a lifetime, you'll descend a 32-foot ladder, crawl through a tunnel, then grapple with more ladders and stone steps. As a prize, you'll get an outstanding view of Soda Canyon.

Park *in* Numbers

369
Area covered (sq miles)

700
Thickness of Carbon Glacier (ft)

14,410
Height of Mt. Rainier (ft)

44

WA

MT. RAINIER NATIONAL PARK

Mt Rainier is a spider's web of hiking trails—more than 260 miles of them, to be exact. We guarantee that they'll lure you in, leaving you with a lifetime love of the outdoors.

Don't let Mt. Rainier's carpets of brightly colored wildflowers fool you into thinking that this national park is all about picturesque nature walks. Mt. Rainier is an active volcano that formed roughly 500,000 years ago. Though its last eruption happened about 1,000 years ago, the volcano is still considered active, meaning that at some point, it will have future eruptions. Today, there is ice where there was fire. There are also 35 square miles of glaciers. Depending on the temperature, the ice slabs move about seven inches a day.

Because of Mt. Rainier's 14,410-foot summit, the park is a mountaineering training ground. Many visiting climbers dream of scaling Mt. Everest, Earth's highest mountain. What future heroes will you meet as you trek Mt. Rainier's trails? Could that hero be you?

Animal lovers will have a blast in this park. If you're hiking the well-trodden paths, you'll likely run across more than one wild creature. You might meet adorable marmots, black bears, ptarmigans, snowshoe hares, foxes, and rabbits. You may also encounter mountain lions and bobcats. Remember the outdoor golden rule—appreciate these carnivores from afar. For the budding botanist in you, plant life includes alpine wildflowers; cedar, fir, hemlock, and pine trees; mushrooms; heather; and huckleberry shrubs. How herbaceous!

A bit of trivia: the stunning Mt. Rainier was named by British navy captain George Vancouver for his friend Rear Admiral Peter Rainier in 1792. Now that's a nice way to honor your BFF.

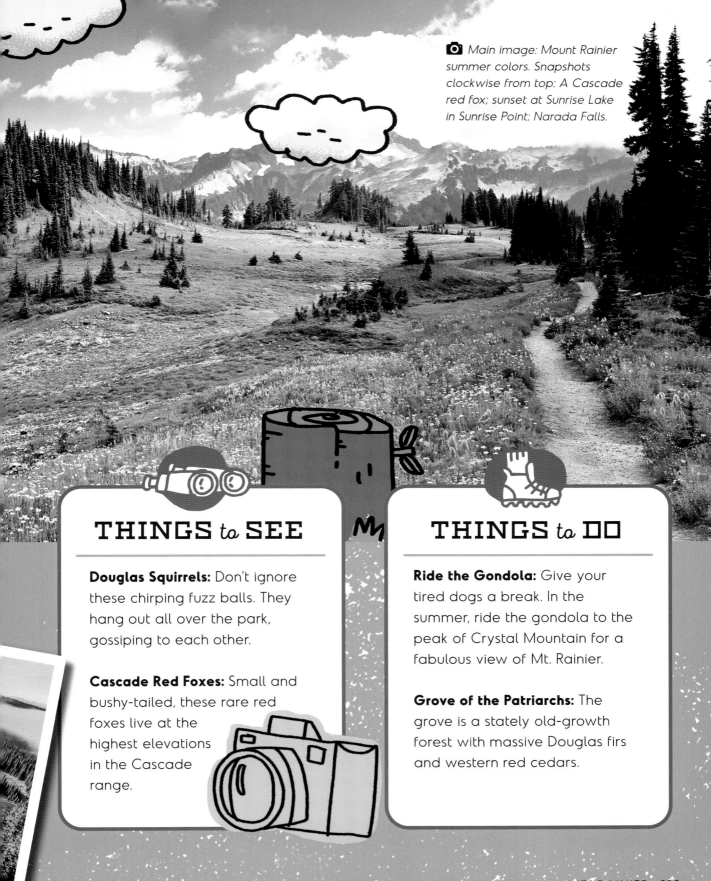

Main image: Mount Rainier summer colors. Snapshots clockwise from top: A Cascade red fox; sunset at Sunrise Lake in Sunrise Point; Narada Falls.

THINGS to SEE

Douglas Squirrels: Don't ignore these chirping fuzz balls. They hang out all over the park, gossiping to each other.

Cascade Red Foxes: Small and bushy-tailed, these rare red foxes live at the highest elevations in the Cascade range.

THINGS to DO

Ride the Gondola: Give your tired dogs a break. In the summer, ride the gondola to the peak of Crystal Mountain for a fabulous view of Mt. Rainier.

Grove of the Patriarchs: The grove is a stately old-growth forest with massive Douglas firs and western red cedars.

Park *in* Numbers

113
Area covered (sq miles)

225–300 million
Age of the New River
(estimated years)

3,030
Length of New River
Gorge Bridge (feet)

45

WV

NEW RIVER GORGE NATIONAL PARK

Nestled in the Appalachian Mountains of West Virginia hides one of the oldest rivers on Earth. Come for the beautiful gorge vistas, stay for the unique history of the American coal and railroad industries.

New River Gorge National Park seems made for adventure. The topography of rugged Appalachian Mountains, steep plateaus, and the powerful river at the center of everything is a playground of rock climbing and white-water rafting. If you're not into extreme sports, a hike to lookouts such as Grandview or Sandstone Falls provides tranquil vistas of the park's central canyon, tall peaks, and lush forests. Evergreen plants such as white pine, hemlock, mountain laurel, ground pine, and rhododendron create a breathtaking forest landscape in winter.

New River Gorge is the deepest river gorge in the Appalachian Mountains. The New River runs along the path of an ancient waterway, the Teays, and is thought to be the second-oldest river in the world. Being old has its advantages: several endemic animal species have evolved here, like the colorful candy darter, a tiny fish that grows to only three inches. The surrounding woods are a refuge for multiple endangered species, including the Virginia big-eared bat and the Indiana bat.

New River Gorge holds other surprises, such as railroad tracks and coal mines. More than 100 years ago, people mined coal and lumber in the gorge, and built the railroad that would transport these materials to meet the demands of industrialization. Some think that this is the real-life setting of *The Ballad of John Henry*, a song about an African American folk hero and railroad worker.

📷 *Main images: Abandoned coal tower (below); Grandview overlook (above right). Snapshots top to bottom: Sandstone Falls; Virginia bat.*

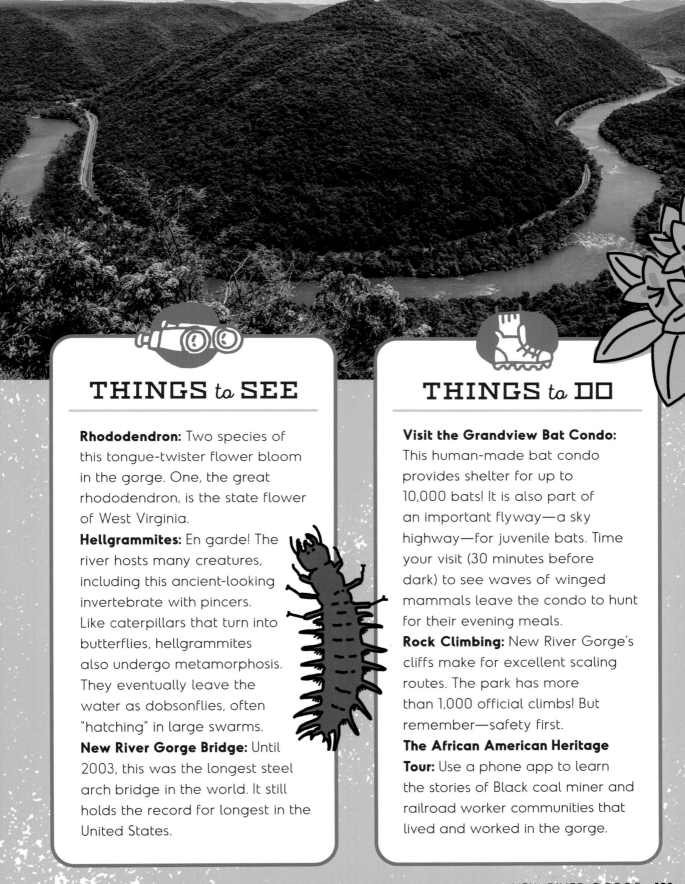

THINGS to SEE

Rhododendron: Two species of this tongue-twister flower bloom in the gorge. One, the great rhododendron, is the state flower of West Virginia.

Hellgrammites: En garde! The river hosts many creatures, including this ancient-looking invertebrate with pincers. Like caterpillars that turn into butterflies, hellgrammites also undergo metamorphosis. They eventually leave the water as dobsonflies, often "hatching" in large swarms.

New River Gorge Bridge: Until 2003, this was the longest steel arch bridge in the world. It still holds the record for longest in the United States.

THINGS to DO

Visit the Grandview Bat Condo: This human-made bat condo provides shelter for up to 10,000 bats! It is also part of an important flyway—a sky highway—for juvenile bats. Time your visit (30 minutes before dark) to see waves of winged mammals leave the condo to hunt for their evening meals.

Rock Climbing: New River Gorge's cliffs make for excellent scaling routes. The park has more than 1,000 official climbs! But remember—safety first.

The African American Heritage Tour: Use a phone app to learn the stories of Black coal miner and railroad worker communities that lived and worked in the gorge.

Park *in* Numbers

1,068
Area covered (sq miles)

9,206
Highest point:
Goode Mountain (ft)

400
Lowest point:
Skagit River (ft)

46

WA

NORTH CASCADES NATIONAL PARK

Have you ever stood in a place, wondering whether anyone else had set foot there before you? If the answer is yes, you'll find a place to call your own in this national park.

PRISTINE.

This 10-dollar word means "clean" and "unspoiled"—and it's the only way to accurately describe North Cascades National Park. The swaths of mountain-crusted land stretch out before you. Dark-green pine forests spread thick as peanut butter over the hills. The whole area looks fresh and perfect, like it belongs inside a snow globe.

An ice factory created this awesome place. The park contains more than 300 glaciers! These ice monsters put the "cascade" in North Cascades. Not only do glaciers supply the rivers and streams with rushing water, the ice giants are also responsible for carving the landscape into high mountains, deep valleys, and bejeweled lakes.

North Cascades isn't completely untouched. In addition to the Native peoples who survived here for thousands of years, archaeologists have identified 260 prehistoric sites, including homesteads, mines, and sheep-farming settlements.

Each visitor gets to decide what meaning they find in the park's raw nature. Risk-takers see adventure in its steep cliff faces. Scientists see an outdoor laboratory where they can study a unique, raw ecosystem to monitor the effects of climate change. What will North Cascades show you?

THINGS to SEE

Wolverines: Yep, wolverines don't only lend their name to your favorite metal-clawed mutant. Keep an eye on the forests, where these muscular animals scavenge.

Chinook Salmon: These fish fight their way up the Skagit River to spawn. They go from blue-green in the ocean to olive brown, red, or purplish in fresh water.

THINGS to DO

North Cascades Institute: The educational programs held at North Cascades Environmental Learning Center will blow your mind! Classes cover everything from animal biology to nature photography.

Picnic at Diablo Lake: Despite its devilish name, Diablo Lake is heavenly. Unpack your lunch at Diablo Lake Overlook after fishing in the turquoise waters.

📷 *Main images: Picture Lake and Mt. Shuksan (above left); a wolverine balances on a tree trunk (below, silhouette). Snapshots top to bottom: Diablo Lake at sunrise; a Chinook salmon.*

Park in Numbers

1,442
Area covered (sq miles)

73
Length of wild coastline (miles)

300
Bird species

47

WA

OLYMPIC NATIONAL PARK

Come one, come all, to the slice of rugged wilderness where three worlds collide: temperate rainforest, coastline, and mountains.

EPIC.

Just like its namesake, Mt. Olympus rises regally from the mists of Olympic National Park—a meeting place for the gods. It makes sense: you can imagine three mythical gods, each ruling a different realm, forging Olympic's wildly different terrains together with their bare hands. First, you have Mt. Olympus itself, among the Olympic range that skirts its peak. From there, the Hoh River flows, giving life to otherworldly patches of emerald-green rainforests, until the river spills out into the vast blue-gray Pacific Ocean. It's not hard to believe that Poseidon still reigns over this long stretch of coastline, which is considered one of the world's most untamed coastal habitats.

The majority of Olympic National Park occupies the center of the remote Olympic Peninsula. The park is near the reservations of several Native American tribes, including the Skokomish, Makah, Hoh, Quinault, Quileute, Jamestown S'Klallam, Port Gamble S'Klallam, and Lower Elwha Klallam. These Native American tribes have remained

📷 *Main image: Deer and mountains. Snapshots top to bottom: A curious Olympic marmot; Sol Duc River cascade and wooden bridge.*

YOWZA!

THINGS to SEE

Olympic Marmots: Found only on the Olympic Peninsula, this marmot is known for being social. Listen for its four distinct whistles! The cat-sized critter will chat your ear off!

Epiphytes: That's the scientific name for an organism that grows on the surface of a plant, such as moss. Olympic is literally covered with them, giving the forest a jungle vibe.

Anadromous Fish: This term refers to fish that migrate from salt water to fresh water to mate. Salmon are especially important: they carry nutrients back and forth from ocean to river.

THINGS to DO

Explore the (Coastal Temperate) Rainforest: A ranger-led nature walk will teach you even more about four rainforests within the park. Bring your raincoat!

Tide Pools: The park's 73 miles of coastline offers plenty of adventure. Mora's Hole-in-the-Wall is a popular tide pool area. Look at (but don't touch) anemones—the flowers of the sea.

Go Sledding: If you visit in the wintertime, there's still plenty to do—like ride the ski lift! The Hurricane Ridge ski and snowboard area offers snowshoeing, skiing, and tubing.

connected to the land and their ancestors, cultures, and traditions. One such tradition is the potlatch, which is both a feast and a social gathering.

Olympic's 73-mile-long coast is a rarity. Its beaches, tide pools, and "sea stacks" are a never-ending explosion of life, including nesting seabirds, seals, whales, anemones, crabs . . . the list goes on. However, Olympic is best known for its otherworldly and downright bizarre primeval forests (in

other words, really, *really* old forests). If you did nothing but hike on the numerous trails, you would still be swept away on a magic carpet ride—and that flying rug would be made entirely of moss, which seems to cover every inch of the landscape. Underneath, you'd see Sitka spruces, western hemlocks, and Douglas firs. You'd swear that the twisty, many-limbed trees strewn with stringy lichens were stolen from the pages of a Dr. Seuss book.

Park in Numbers

346
Area covered (sq miles)

650+
Number of Newspaper Rock petroglyphs

1250-1380
Human occupation of Puerco Pueblo (CE)

48

AZ

PETRIFIED
FOREST
NATIONAL
PARK

Have you imagined traveling through time? Then this park may be just right for you! A visit here feels like a trip back to the Triassic period.

MAP

Have you heard of the Crystal Forest? No, we didn't make that up. Despite its awesome name, the fossilized logs scattered over the ground look like plain ol' rocks at first glance. But as you stare, you'll begin to see things. Shifting colors. Glittering flecks . . . Be patient. Be curious. A stroll down the Crystal Forest Trail will reveal hidden kaleidoscopes of fiery reds, oranges, and purples.

Like mummies, the trees were preserved by a natural process more than 210 million years ago. The trees were washed into a river and buried in sediment. Minerals in the sediment, including silica from volcanic ash, seeped into the wood over time, turning the wood to stone, or petrified wood.

At sunset, brilliant colors melt over the Painted Desert's horizon, imitating the fossilized trees' magic. But only the twinkling stars are as beautiful—and as old—as the ancient crystals contained within.

THINGS to SEE

Newspaper Rock: Named for the petroglyphs left by Ancestral Puebloans, Newspaper Rock has scrawled clan names and calendar events.

📷 *Main images: The Crystal Forest (left); sunbathing lizard (below). Snapshots clockwise from top: Striped purple sandstone formations of the Blue Mesa badlands; petroglyphs on Newspaper Rock; petrified wood.*

THINGS to DO

Rainbow Forest Museum: Here, you can learn more about petrified wood fossils. View the remains of the prehistoric animals who roamed here!

Park in Numbers

41.6
Area covered (sq miles)

3,304
Highest elevation:
North Chalone Peak (ft)

347
Wild California condors
left in the world

49

PINNACLES
NATIONAL
PARK

For being so tiny, this park carries a megaton of personality in its craggy volcanic peaks, towering spires, and dazzling wildlife.

A STEGOSAURUS-LIKE SPINE OF ROCKS SHOOTS UP THROUGH THE GROUND.

CHIRP.

his is only the start of Pinnacles's legendary topography, the shape of its land. A brown-and-green ocean of peaks, canyons, spires, and caves, the park will knock your socks off.

The strangest thing about Pinnacles? It was dragged here. The park was once an ancient volcano almost 200 miles away. But little by little, tectonic plate activity slowly pulled the volcano to its current location—and at one inch every year, it's still on the move.

Pinnacles makes up for its small size by sheltering a huge array of wildlife. The park has dainty ladybugs, giant condors, and everything in between! Look skyward for golden eagles or American kestrels circling the park's high cliffs. The caves house more than half of the bat species found in California.

To the west of superstars like Yosemite and Death Valley, this desert gem often gets ignored. Trust us: Pinnacles really is tops.

📷 *Main image: Landscape filled with volcanic rocks. Snapshots top to bottom: California scrub jay; Pinnacles National Park.*

THINGS to SEE

Townsend's Big-Eared Bats: Immediately recognizable by its long ears (reminiscent of the jackrabbit's), this brown bat roosts in talus caves.

THINGS to DO

Caving: Talus caves are great for spelunkers in training. Just remember to bring your flashlight!

Park *in* Numbers

206
Area covered (sq miles)

380
Height of Hyperion (ft)

45%
California's remaining old-growth redwoods protected here

50

CA

REDWOOD NATIONAL & STATE PARKS

Was there a time when you would have traded anything for your own peaceful paradise? Your search is over—you'll find calm, quiet, and so much more when you lose yourself in this expansive forest of sky-high sentinels. So leave your woes behind, slap on your walking shoes, and join us!

F oggy forests sprawl. Fern groves, plucked from a prehistoric era, sway. Four-legged, antlered creatures rear up, three times your height. Blocking out the sun with a thick, green canopy, the world's tallest trees rocket up hundreds of feet in the air—and blanket the earth below in silence.

We're not describing the next blockbuster movie about dinosaurs. We're talking about Redwoods National and State Parks, where 40 rugged miles of old-growth redwoods will lead you on a path to self-discovery. Towering above like wooden skyscrapers, the coast redwood trees are more than 90 times taller—and hundreds, even *thousands*, of years older—than you are. Here, you'll exercise your legs and your imagination. Allow the cool, wet temperate rainforest climate and the rows of gigantic *Sequoia sempervirens* to fill your head with velociraptors and tyrannosaurs.

You wouldn't be totally off the mark, either. Fossil evidence proves that the redwoods flourished during the height of the Jurassic period, 160 million years ago.

Every year, the lush green canopy gets up to 140 inches of rain. The moisture, along with rich forest-floor soil and the trees' natural capabilities, makes it possible for the redwoods to gracefully grow and age. What have these mysterious, ancient trees witnessed? If they could speak, what would they tell us?

This park isn't only a safe haven for trees—it's also is a refuge for many species on the brink of extinction. Threatened animals like Chinook salmon spawn in its freshwater streams, while Steller's sea lions gather on the coastal rocks. California spotted owls find safety on perches high in the piney branches. Condors, which hadn't been seen in the redwoods for more than a century, were reintroduced to the park in 2022. It's as if the redwoods, huddled together in the mist, once again agreed to give shelter to their endangered friends.

A certain green-eared and white-robed master would be right at home among the redwoods, where tranquility is as thick as stew. Visit, you must!

THINGS to SEE

Coast Redwoods: This isn't the largest or oldest species in California—that title belongs to another type of sequoia called *Sequoiadendron giganteum*—but it's definitely the tallest.

Roosevelt Elk: North America's largest elk munch on grasses, other plants, and berries. Just goes to show you: eat your vegetables, kids!

THINGS to DO

Lady Bird Johnson Grove Trail: This short nature walk is marked with helpful signs that tell you all about the ecology of the redwoods.

Elk Meadow and Trillium Falls: If you're lucky, you'll spy elk grazing on your trek to Trillium Falls, a half-mile hike through the redwoods.

Park in Numbers

415
Area covered (sq miles)

77
Number of peaks higher
than 12,000 ft

355
Miles of hiking trails

51

CO

ROCKY MOUNTAIN NATIONAL PARK

Like a scene from an epic Norse myth, the vista includes peaks slathered in glistening white snow and encircled by thousands of acres of deep-green forest. The god of thunder would be at home in this corner of Colorado. Rocky Mountain is the stuff legends are made of.

LEGENDARY.

The Never Summer Wilderness. The Mummy Range. Wild Basin. These aren't the titles of adventure novels—they're the names of mountain ranges, lakes, and regions within Rocky Mountain National Park. You'll have to travel deep within America, all the way to landlocked Colorado, to discover this high-altitude behemoth. But the trip is worth it. Coming upon Rocky Mountain feels like reaching for the trophy at the center of a maze.

Though the terrain is thrilling in all seasons, Rocky Mountain is best-dressed during the winter. While many possible adventures are too rugged for inexperienced hikers, you don't have to scale a sky-high summit to mine the park's rewards. Inhale crisp, clean mountain air as your eyes drink in a vista stained purple by the setting sun. Enjoy a quiet moment nestled in fir and spruce forests. Wave across the tundra at a herd of moose or bighorn sheep as they show off their antlered and horned heads.

This alpine dreamland is an adventure waiting to be lived. A snowball itching to be thrown. A powdered hill begging for its sled and rider. A mirrored lake that will reflect your wildest dreams. Now, all you have to do is look.

THINGS to SEE

Bighorn Sheep: The park's official symbol, these mammals are well named. Their curved brown horns are quite large. They can also scale a rock face better than any professional climber.

Quaking Aspens: When the ground is covered in snow, the aspens' white bark sometimes blends in with the landscape. But in the fall, you can't miss their trembling bouquets of leaves.

THINGS to DO

Snowshoe the Winter Trails: Tie on a pair of moose-sized snowshoes and glide over the snow. As you float along forested trails, keep an eye out for large mammals like mule deer and elk.

Lily Lake Trail: This nature trail loops around the scenic Lily Lake. It's easy to walk, and it's the perfect place to view abundant wildflowers and a bounty of birds in the warmer months.

📷 *Main images: Rocky Mountain Lake (opposite); bighorn sheep (silhouette below). Snapshots top to bottom: Colorful forest; Aspen sunset.*

Park in Numbers

143
Area covered (sq miles)

25
Species of cactus

8,666
Highest point (ft)

52
AZ

SAGUARO
NATIONAL
PARK

*Here, all trails lead to
the saguaro. If the desert
is a stage, then this
colossal, prickly cactus
is its star.*

Main images: Sunset at Saguaro (top left); dirt road in Saguaro (bottom right). Snapshot: A javelina.

YOU'D RECOGNIZE THESE CHARISMATIC CACTI IN A SECOND, PILGRIM.

Saguaros are Hollywood famous, immortalized in movies, art, and images as symbols of the American West. And Saguaro National Park was created to protect them—the first park ever to be based on a specific plant.

There's something human about these cacti. With sturdy trunks and thick arms, saguaros posture like bodyguards for the roadrunners, Gila monsters, and javelinas that scamper below. These mighty plants can weigh eight tons and grow up to 50 feet, but progress is slow. It can take 35 years for a saguaro to produce its first night-blooming flower and 60 to 70 years to grown its first arm!

Warning! It is illegal to harm or move a saguaro. This rule protects you, not the cactus. If it falls, a single branch weighs enough to cause serious harm.

THINGS to SEE

Javelinas: These bristle-haired desert dwellers are neither wild pigs nor massive rodents. They're peccaries. Just remember—Peter Piper picked a pack of peccaries.

THINGS to DO

Junior Ranger Day Camp: There are excellent junior ranger programs in every park, but this camp is offered year-round. Rangers hike and study in the desert.

Park *in* **Numbers**

631
Area covered (sq miles)

52,508
Volume of General
Sherman tree (cu ft)

14,491
Height of Mt. Whitney (ft)

53

CA

SEQUOIA NATIONAL PARK

Red-skinned trees soar as high as the birds nesting in their green, broom-thistled branches. Craning your neck to see their tops, you'll think nothing could rise taller. Then, in the distance, your eyes land on a majestic mountain that stands guard over all. Its jagged peaks poke through the clouds, ripping the sky apart.

HOW'S THE AIR UP THERE?

HERE BE GIANTS.

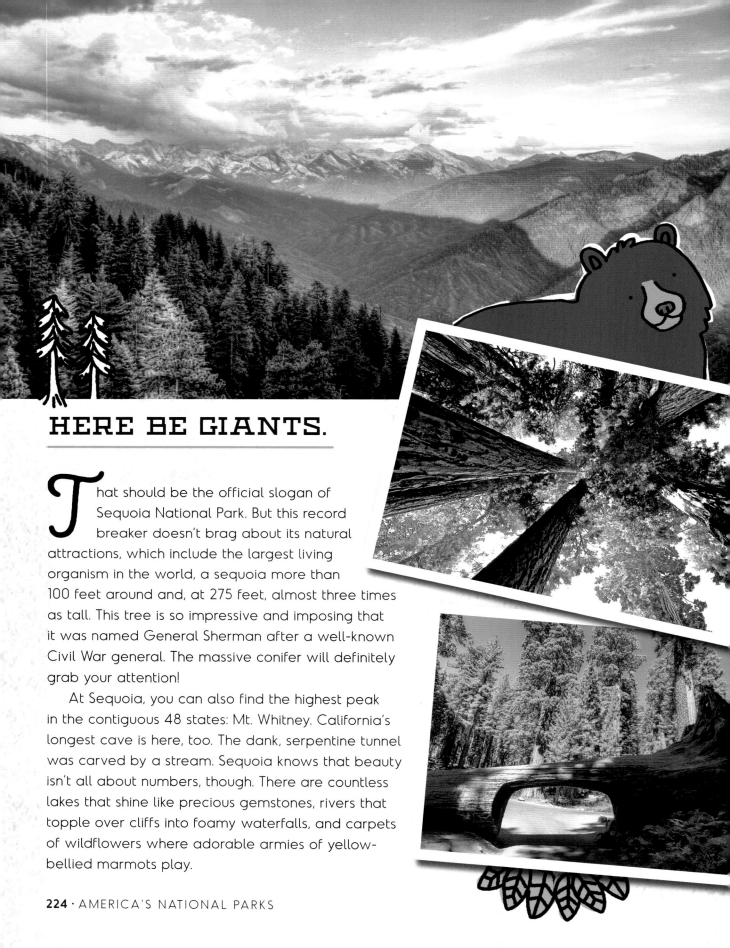

That should be the official slogan of Sequoia National Park. But this record breaker doesn't brag about its natural attractions, which include the largest living organism in the world, a sequoia more than 100 feet around and, at 275 feet, almost three times as tall. This tree is so impressive and imposing that it was named General Sherman after a well-known Civil War general. The massive conifer will definitely grab your attention!

At Sequoia, you can also find the highest peak in the contiguous 48 states: Mt. Whitney. California's longest cave is here, too. The dank, serpentine tunnel was carved by a stream. Sequoia knows that beauty isn't all about numbers, though. There are countless lakes that shine like precious gemstones, rivers that topple over cliffs into foamy waterfalls, and carpets of wildflowers where adorable armies of yellow-bellied marmots play.

THINGS to SEE

Black Bears: Don't let the shuffling, lumbering gait of the black bear fool you: they can reach speeds of up to 30 miles per hour. Black bears are also great swimmers and climbers. Observe them from a distance . . . and don't run a triathlon against them.

Giant Sequoias: These colossal trees have superpowers! Their thick bark helps insulate them from wildfires. Tannin in their bark protects the trees from insects and fungus. Scout for General Sherman standing at attention among his army of giants.

THINGS to DO

Caving: Crystal Cave sounds like something from a video game, but the only obstacles you'll have to watch for in this real-life, 10,000-year-old cave are stalactites, stalagmites, hanging veils of ghostly marble . . . and maybe the occasional bat or spider.

Swimming: When the summer rolls in over the hilly landscape, cannonball into one of the stunning swimming holes near Potwisha and Hospital Rock. But first, ask a ranger if the water levels are low enough for safe splashing!

SPLASH!

We don't play favorites, but we're pretty sure that the heart of this park can be found in Giant Forest, where you'll find stands of sequoia trees rising up from the ground like the thick legs of a thousand dinosaurs. Covering the massive trunks, the trees' distinctive reddish bark resembles strips of bacon. Sequoias are extremely rare—they grow only here, on the western slope of the Sierra Nevada range, where the unique conditions are just right. And boy, do these trees know how to *live*—a single sequoia can thrive for more than 3,000 years.

In 1890, Sequoia National Park was created by the U.S. Congress to protect the sequoias from logging (chopping down trees for wood). Sadly, before the park was protected, many of these gentle giants were destroyed. We have heroes to thank for the sights you can visit today: the first park rangers to guard these giants were African American regiments of Buffalo Soldiers from the U.S. Army Cavalry.

📷 *Main image: Sequoia National Park. Snapshots from top to bottom: Looking up at giant sequoias; a tunnel cut from a fallen tree.*

Park *in* Numbers

308.5
Area covered (sq miles)

8
Rare plant species

93
Height of Overall Run,
highest waterfall (ft)

54
VA
SHENANDOAH NATIONAL PARK

Forget roller coasters. Forget race cars. You're cruising Skyline Drive, the 105-mile road that curves along the jagged spine of Virginia's Blue Ridge Mountains. Rush to the finish line, where the black-ribbon road leads to never-ending forests and vivid wildflowers. Buckle up.

It's no mystery why city dwellers flock to Shenandoah National Park. Located just two hours away from Washington, D.C., Shenandoah is a weekend escape for people wanting to lose themselves in a natural dreamscape of forest, wetlands, rivers, and mountains. However, the name Shenandoah is a riddle in and of itself. Many believe that it has Native American origins and means "silver waters" or "daughter of the stars."

Compared to other eastern old-growth forests, the symphony of maple, birch, ash, and basswood trees that make up much of Shenandoah's woods are quite young. Why? When European colonizers arrived in the area in the 18th century, they razed the ancient forests in order to build farmsteads, mills, and orchards along the slopes. When the government finally decided to create the park in the 1930s, they planted trees and other plants to replace farmland and logged forests. Today, more than 100 cemeteries are the only remaining evidence of those settlers. However, the 1,046 species of plant life still face risks. Invasive gypsy moths have destroyed large numbers of oak trees. You can see the barkless trees along the road. And a disease called blight has damaged chestnut trees.

Today, Shenandoah is an excellent park for family camping. There are plenty of cabins available, where you can roast marshmallows over ranger-approved fire pits. These homes away from home are located near some of the park's best hiking trails, such as Limberlost and Fox Hollow, where you can explore rock formations eroded by powerful storms, breathe in the scent of blooming mountain laurel, splash in waterfalls, and nibble on the fruits of wild blackberry bushes (a black bear's favorite meal). After traipsing through the pine, oak, hickory, and poplar forests, rest your weary legs in Big Meadows. The popular wildlife-viewing spot is often overrun by white-tailed deer, wild turkeys, red-tailed hawks, and, sometimes, black bears. Watch as migrating birds land on the branches above. They, too, will be resting in preparation for their own epic journey over the Blue Ridge Mountains.

📷 *Main images: Shenandoah Valley during golden hour (top left); a bobcat stalks prey (near right); autumn in White Oak Canyon (far right). Snapshot: Blue Ridge Mountains from Little Stony Man Cliffs.*

THINGS to SEE

Carolina Chickadees: Tune in your ears to the call of chicka-dee-dee-dee, chicka-dee-dee-dee, and you might be lucky enough to spot these tiny birds. They're as cute as cartoons!

Bobcats: There's no guarantee that you'll see one of these elusive, fearsome felines, which is the only large cat species found in the park. If you do spot one, remain at a distance. This kitty's got claws.

THINGS to DO

Luray Caverns: Pull up your chairs for nature's symphony. This vast cavern contains a "Great Stalacpipe Organ," a human-made instrument that plays melodies on the cave's stalactites.

Hike Fox Hollow: Follow the 1.2-mile loop along the crumbling remains of homesteads and flower-decorated valleys. It's especially good for bird-watching. Pack your binoculars!

GIVE ME SPACE.

Park *in* Numbers

110
Area covered (sq miles)

2,865
Height of highest point:
Peck Hill (ft)

200-500
Optimal size of the park's
bison population

55

THEODORE ROOSEVELT NATIONAL PARK

A former president of the United States once called this park "a land of vast, silent spaces, of lonely rivers, and of plains where the wild game stared at the passing horseman." That untamed spirit of wilderness still lives in the rugged hills and fertile floodplains of one of the country's most majestic parks.

AS WITH ANY JUNGLE OR TRUE WILDERNESS, THEODORE ROOSEVELT NATIONAL PARK HOSTS FAR MORE ANIMALS THAN PEOPLE.

HOWDY.

Main image: Sunrise over Theodore Roosevelt National Park. Snapshots top to bottom: A chubby black-tailed prairie dog; feral horses graze in a field.

Stuffed full of bison, feral horses, elk, bighorn sheep, pronghorn, white-tailed deer, mule deer, prairie dogs, and nearly 200 species of birds, the wilds may *look* lonely but the land is hopping, squawking, and clip-clopping with wildlife. There are plenty of jaw-dropping natural wonders, too. Rippling in the breeze, hardy grasslands provide feasts for four-legged creatures (and hiding places for rattlesnakes). Ancient petrified forests are walkable fossil records that lead you on a journey through time.

In 1883, this slice of North Dakota's badlands was a future president's playground. While hunting, hiking, and exploring the grass-covered plains and snaking rivers, Theodore Roosevelt indulged a lifelong love: the land itself. His passion for the rugged outdoors—and the countless hours he spent roaming here—inspired his later conservation efforts, which helped shape the entire national park system. While he was in the White House from 1901 to 1909, he protected 230 million acres of American wilderness. Under Roosevelt's authority, five new national parks were founded.

So—how will this sprawling sea of green inspire you?

THINGS to SEE

Porcupines: These wily badland residents can often be spotted along the park's roads during the night. Their favorite snack? Twigs.

Wild Horses: Think of these horses as freedom seekers. Their once-tame ancestors were brought here in the 1500s by Spanish colonizers—but the horses shrugged off their riders to establish independent herds.

THINGS to DO

Wildlife Viewing: Prairie dogs, bison, and elk can easily be seen from the comfort and safety of your car. With a pair of binoculars, you're good to go!

Junior Ranger Program: You can earn a ranger badge by completing activities in a Junior Ranger booklet while driving along one of the park's scenic routes.

Park *in* Numbers

20
Area covered (sq miles)

300,000+
Number of visitors per year

300+
Species of fish in
the park's waters

56

VI

VIRGIN ISLANDS NATIONAL PARK

Just east of Puerto Rico sits a treasure chest of emerald mountains, sugar-white sands, and reef-crowned seas. Lock yourself inside and throw away the key.

In this paradise of a national park, life is a breeze. Or maybe it's a wave? That sounds right, because 40% of Virgin Islands National Park is under shimmering crystal-clear waters. Here, snorkeling, swimming, diving, and boating are just part of the package.

In the park's vast underwater crab-doms, living reefs reel with tropical fish that make yummy snacks for passing dolphins and sea turtles. Witness the circle of life when you dive underwater, kicking your flippers over gardens of swaying seagrass. *There!* A spotted eagle ray flies through the Caribbean current. *There!* A century-old sea turtle waves its flipper. Below you, bright elkhorn corals, pillar corals, and mountainous star corals decorate the world's largest fish tank: the ocean.

If you don't like to swim, practice your sandcastle architecture or meander through the land-based section of the park, where many ecosystems await. Forests, salt ponds, cactus scrublands, and mangroves are full of plant and animal life. Get out your easel to capture the swirling colors of the pale beaches, dark hidden coves, and aqua water.

Sadly, the islands bear a long history of violence against its native Carib and Taino people. Christopher Columbus's legacy led to the establishment of sugar and cotton plantations, all run using the labor of enslaved people. In the 1700s, one of the first slave rebellions in the Americas occurred here, but it would take another 100 years for slavery to be abolished. To appreciate Native culture, go to the Visitor Center, where artifacts are on display.

📷 *Main image: Reef Bay. Snapshots from top: Bananaquit bird; Annaberg Plantation; two sea stars at Leinster Bay.*

THINGS to SEE

Mangroves: Got your roots in a bunch? These trees appear to be standing on their tippy-toes! Peer underwater to see how they double as a nursery for fish, including young sharks.

Bananaquits: Flitting from flower to feeder, bananaquits will make your day with their cheerful call. The yellow-bellied birds are all over, even on the state seal.

THINGS to DO

Snorkeling: Grab your fins, mask, and snorkel to experience an underwater carnival that never closes. Iridescent fish and other marine life whirl around the colorful coral.

Beach Hopping: As you hop from beach to beach, let the tide wash your troubles away. Or just sleep off your worries in the snow-colored sand.

Park *in* **Numbers**

341
Area covered (sq miles)

655
Total length of shoreline (miles)

500+
Number of islands

ARE YOU SEEING THIS?

VOYAGEURS NATIONAL PARK

If you've ever fantasized about becoming a mermaid, visiting the watery wonderland found in one of America's most mesmerizing national parks would be a dream come true.

ℰstablished almost 50 years ago, the park might not be very old, but the land is old, at least in some places. Perch on layers of two-billion-year-old greenstone. That's half the age of Earth! However, water is the park's show-stopping attraction. Its four major lakes—Rainy, Kabetogama, Namakan, and Sand Point—and over 500 smaller lakes cover 40% of the land. Below their calm surfaces swim the walleyes, Minnesota's most famous freshwater fish.

If you're a landlubber there's still plenty to do and see in the humongous Kabetogama Peninsula wilderness. Shade your eyes against the sun as you observe bald eagles stalking their prey. They perch on stately pines like regal tree toppers. As dusk falls, tune in to the loons calling to one another. Their hauntingly beautiful cries echo from one lake to the next.

In winter, the park morphs into a snowy wonderland. The stretch of white may appear empty, but if you scour the horizon's milky blankness, you might glimpse a pack of gray wolves charging across a frozen lake. If you're lucky, you may also see the spectacular northern lights, which flash green on the horizon. We dare you to explore Voyageurs by ski or snowshoe. Is ice fishing worth braving some of the coldest temperatures in the lower 48 states? As Minnesotans say—*you betcha!*

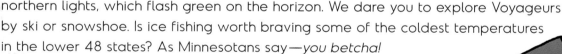

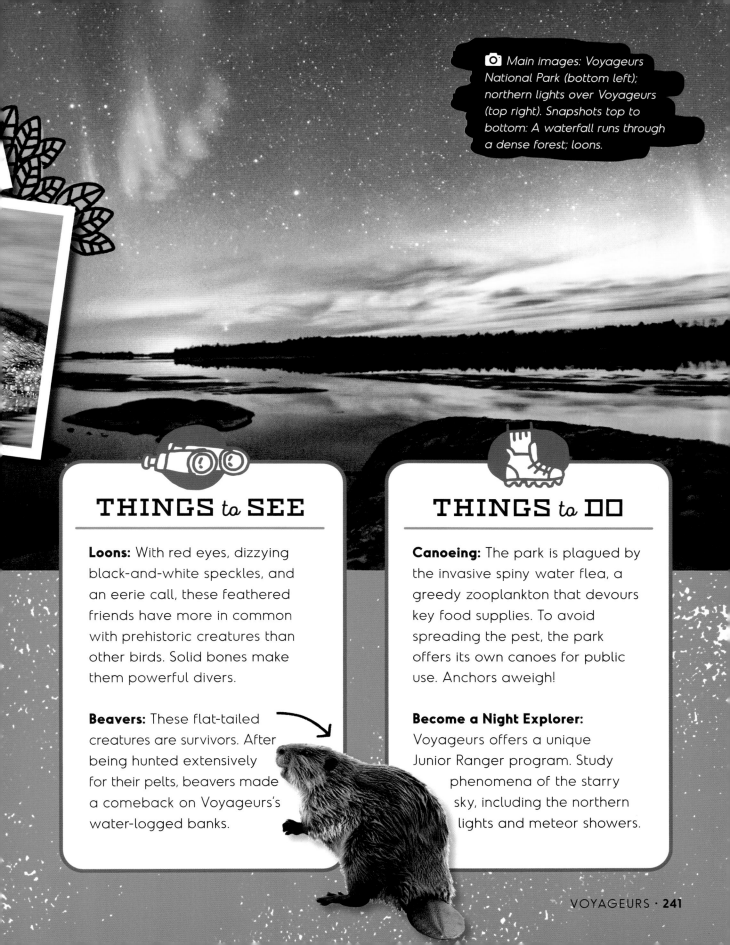

THINGS to SEE

Loons: With red eyes, dizzying black-and-white speckles, and an eerie call, these feathered friends have more in common with prehistoric creatures than other birds. Solid bones make them powerful divers.

Beavers: These flat-tailed creatures are survivors. After being hunted extensively for their pelts, beavers made a comeback on Voyageurs's water-logged banks.

THINGS to DO

Canoeing: The park is plagued by the invasive spiny water flea, a greedy zooplankton that devours key food supplies. To avoid spreading the pest, the park offers its own canoes for public use. Anchors aweigh!

Become a Night Explorer: Voyageurs offers a unique Junior Ranger program. Study phenomena of the starry sky, including the northern lights and meteor showers.

Park in Numbers

228
Area covered (sq miles)

150°F
Highest sand surface temperatures

30
Size of the largest
dunefield (sq miles)

WHITE SANDS NATIONAL PARK

Welcome to the world's largest gypsum dunefield. Follow the fossilized footprints of dire wolves, giant sloths, and our human ancestors back in time to the last ice age, 20,000 years ago.

Ho ho—huh? The powdery white hills in the Tularosa Basin aren't piles of snow—they're sand! These sparkling dunes are made of gypsum. The name might sound fanciful, but believe it or not, you're already familiar with this mineral. It's in most sidewalk chalk. Gypsum, however, rarely exists naturally as sand, making this park's geology unique. To add another dash of magic, gypsum also crystallizes as selenite. You can see these jagged crystals jutting out of the ground at Lake Lucero.

Can you picture what White Sands looked like 20,000 years ago? Its incredible fossil record is an excellent cheat sheet. Fossilized footprints paint a picture of megafauna such as mammoths, giant sloths, and American lions that once roamed alongside humans in a much wetter, greener environment. According to paleontologists, one incredible set of ancient human prints preserved here tells the story of a woman carrying a toddler across the once moist and muddy terrain.

📷 *Main images: Construction of the NASA White Sands Test Facility in 1963 (opposite); jagged crystals of selenite (below). Snapshot: Bleached earless lizard (above).*

THINGS to SEE

Cacti: These hardy plants survive—and thrive—in the harsh conditions of the Chihuahuan Desert. Observe New Mexico agave, soaptree yucca, claret cup cactus, ocotillo, and many more cacti and succulents in their natural habitat.

White Animals: Can you spy the many species that evolved to match their white gypsum surroundings? Start with the sand wolf spider, bleached earless lizard, and Apache pocket mouse.

THINGS to DO

Interdune Boardwalk: Take a leisurely stroll down this boardwalk, which offers the best views of the dunefield.

Become a Tracker: In addition to fossilized footprints, the sand dunes also capture animal tracks daily. Can you identify the local wildlife by just their prints?

Sledding: Fly down the dunes on a plastic saucer. Just don't forget sunscreen!

More than perhaps any other park, White Sands is a cross-section of human history—the good, the bad, and the ugly. The park is a document of our evolution, our fight for survival, Spanish colonization, and our exploration of outer space. The park contains a NASA rocket engine testing site and space shuttle runway. A missile range operated by the U.S. government is also nearby.

Park in Numbers

52.9
Area covered (sq miles)

150
Miles of the cave that have
been mapped

500–550
Number of bison

59

SD

WIND CAVE
NATIONAL
PARK

In the Black Hills of South Dakota, beneath the hooves of shaggy bison, a seemingly endless cave slumbers under the earth.

HIYA!

Wind Cave is mostly an underground universe. A galaxy of explored passageways that lead to . . . well, we don't exactly know. Like outer space, Wind Cave's tunnels draw you farther into darkness until they end in chilly black holes—and mystery.

Which is precisely why Wind Cave is so much fun to explore! Approximately 150 miles have been mapped to date, though the caves seem to stretch into infinity. What you *can* see will keep you entertained. Intricate boxwork formations crawl over the ceiling like an oversized spiderweb. Sixty to 100 million years old, the ancient calcite threads are seen almost nowhere else on the planet.

📷 *Main images: A bison herd in the grasslands above the cave complex (below); lit surfaces in Wind Cave National Park (top right). Snapshots clockwise from top: A cave tunnel; a black-footed ferret; boxwork formation on rock.*

THINGS to SEE

Black-Footed Ferrets: These nocturnal hunters mainly eat prairie dogs. They were thought to be extinct, but a small population was discovered and soon reintroduced into the park!

THINGS to DO

Cave Tours: The 490-foot-deep Wind Cave is this park's star attraction. There are many guided tours to choose from!

But wait. There's more! The cave actually breathes. In and out, in and out, like a snoozing subterranean monster. If you prefer a more scientific explanation, the breathing is the air pressure equalizing inside and outside the cave. Either way, our spidey senses are tingling!

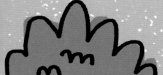

Park *in* Numbers

20,625
Area covered (sq miles)

18,008
Height of Mt. St. Elias (ft)

1,500
Weight of the largest
grizzly bears (lb)

60

AK

WRANGELL-ST. ELIAS NATIONAL PARK & PRESERVE

Whites, grays, greens, yellows, and blues swirl together like paint to depict one of the world's last great frontiers. Fall off the map in America's largest national park.

THERE IS NO BIGGER ADVENTURE THAN WRANGELL-ST. ELIAS NATIONAL PARK.

*L*iterally. With 13.2 million—*million*—acres, Wrangell is the largest national park in the entire country. It's six times the size of Yellowstone.

But why stop there? Combine Wrangell with its U.S. neighbor, Glacier Bay National Park, and Kluane National Park and Reserve and Tatshenshini-Alsek Provincial Park in Canada—and voilà—you have the largest protected wilderness in the entire world. If giants roamed the park's ground, even they would be dwarfed by the sheer scale of Wrangell's wild features. Nine of the 16 highest mountain summits in the United States are found here, including towering Mt. St. Elias.

Given the park's grandness, it makes sense that it boasts a wide variety of terrains. Adventurers can choose from peaks, glaciers, dense spruce forests, and a steaming volcano laced in ice. The wildlife is just as diverse. Dall sheep frolic, their coarse white fur blending in with the snow. Moose root around bog willows. Grizzly bears swipe their massive claws through the salmon-filled

Copper River, hoping for dinner. The park once held more literal treasures, too. Below its four mountain ranges, thousands of workers once mined stores of valuable gold and copper. Visit one of the early 20th-century mining towns to learn more about what lies beneath.

Journeying through Wrangell is the work of a lifetime. But that doesn't mean you shouldn't try. If you take a chance on this national park, you'll definitely strike gold.

THINGS to SEE

Bald Eagles: Soaring overhead like a beacon of freedom, these elegant birds of prey love to coast over the riversides.

Salmon: Many salmon run in these rivers. They're a critical food source for Alaskan natives and brown bears.

THINGS to DO

Flightseeing: The only way to take in the Wrangell's sprawling, unrivaled epicness is from the air. Take to the skies for a once-in-a-lifetime flightseeing tour.

Travel the McCarthy Road: You can drive along this historic train route, which stretches for 60 miles. The plentiful lookouts are breathtaking.

AWWOOOO

Park *in* Numbers

3,472
Area covered (sq miles)

1,063
Number of grizzly bears

300+
Height of highest geyser
eruption, Steamboat (ft)

61

ID MT WY

YELLOWSTONE NATIONAL PARK

Have you ever dreamed of climbing a volcano? Do you stay up all night wondering what it would be like to roam alongside a wild pack of prehistoric beasts? Or are you busy practicing your astronaut skills so you can visit another planet one day? Good news! At Yellowstone National Park, you can do all three. Maybe even before lunch.

HI

Yellowstone is weird. Like, *really* weird. It's filled with geysers that spew streams of hissing water into the air. These large craters look like the blowholes of humongous whales—and they're everywhere! Also, watch out for rainbow-colored hot springs that could boil potatoes. Not bizarre enough for you? Be careful of cracks in the ground that belch steam. Standing next to one of these steam vents is like bumping into a burping dragon. Sure, you'll also find pretty waterfalls and fields blooming with wildflowers—the park is so big that many people drive through it to see every inch of the beautiful landscape. But with blasts of molten air and giant puddles of bubbling mud soup, this is one extraordinary park.

📷 *Main image: Bison in the Lamar Valley. Snapshots clockwise from top: A grizzly crosses the road; Lower Yellowstone Falls; Grand Prismatic Spring.*

CHEESE!

THINGS to SEE

Bison: Yellowstone has approximately 5,900 bison, which have grazed here since prehistoric times. President Barack Obama declared these car-sized beasts the national mammal in 2016.

Gray Wolf: Gray wolves almost became extinct after being killed by ranchers in the 1900s. Now, there are more than 100 howling wolves in the park. Awoooooo!

Grizzly Bear: In summer, grizzlies are easiest to spot in meadows. Try spying on them in Lamar Valley. These clever bears sometimes cause traffic jams on the road!

THINGS to DO

Become a Junior Ranger: Go on a short ranger-led hike or listen to a wildlife talk around a ranger's campfire. Ask rangers *anything* about the park.

Geyser Watching: These superheated spouts can shoot water more than 100 feet high. Old Faithful shoots 3,700 to 8,400 gallons of water with each blast. On average, it erupts every 93 minutes!

Grand Prismatic Spring: This acidic hot spring looks like a melted rainbow. And it's HUGE— almost as big as a football field.

Why is Yellowstone boiling like a witch's cauldron? Easy—because it *is* a cauldron. The Yellowstone cauldron, or caldera, was created by a supervolcano that erupted millions of years ago. That's right. When you visit the park, you are standing on top of a *super*volcano. (You can probably guess that a supervolcano is what scientists call a very big volcano.) While the volcano hasn't erupted in over 640,000 years, that doesn't mean it's cooled off. The fiery magma far beneath the ground creates more than 10,000 geysers, hot springs, and boiling mud pits on the surface of the park. Walking through Yellowstone is like exploring an alien planet. There are more geysers in Yellowstone than anywhere else on Earth.

Yellowstone was the world's first national park. President Ulysses S. Grant made it official in 1872 after countless travelers told him stories of this strange

IT'S OFFICIAL!

GRANT

and marvelous land. However, its history is much, much longer than that. Eleven thousand years before tourists were driving cars through it, Native Americans hunted, fished, and performed important ceremonies at the feet of the geysers and springs of Yellowstone. Visiting Yellowstone is the adventure of a lifetime!

📷 *Main images: Old Faithful (far left); a gray wolf pack (below).*

Park in Numbers

1,187
Area covered (sq miles)

1890
Year the park was established

2,425
Height of
Yosemite Falls (ft)

62

CA

YOSEMITE NATIONAL PARK

At the end of a shadowy tunnel lies 759,620 acres of glacier-carved wilderness and rainbow-strung skies— magic barely contained in one of the oldest national parks in the United States.

THE FIRST GLIMPSE OF YOSEMITE VALLEY WILL MAKE YOU GASP.

On one side, Bridalveil Fall flows over steep cliffs, pounding the rocks below with literally tons of force. On the other side, El Capitan—the world's largest granite monolith—stands 3,000 feet tall. Behind this collage of mountain peaks, pristine alpine lakes shine and the curved stone claw of Half Dome beckons. From every angle, Yosemite is picture-perfect. Nature has been working on its artful landscape for hundreds of millions of years.

Yosemite is nestled in the Sierra Nevada, a mountain range that some call "California's backbone." Look at the behemoth sequoia trees in Mariposa Grove. Take your binoculars on a trip along the rivers Tuolumne or Merced—you might find black bears, deer, coyotes, skinks, raccoons, and foxes coexisting on the rich banks. Not long ago, entomologists (scientists who study insects) discovered two brand-new insect species here! What might you detect hiding within the swaying grasses or wedged between the crevices in the glacier-cut land?

📷 Main images: Half Dome at night (above); Vernal Fall along the Mist Trail (opposite). Snapshots top to bottom: Yosemite National Park; a friendly marmot on Mt. Hoffmann.

THINGS to SEE

Sierra Nevada Bighorn Sheep:
These endangered animals are
rarely spotted, but Yosemite is a
place where miracles happen.
Visit craggy areas, keeping your
eyes open for their white rumps.

Sierra Mountain Kingsnakes: With
red, black, and cream colored
bands, kingsnakes got style.
Don't confuse the similar-looking
venomous coral
snakes for them.

THINGS to DO

Swimming: Splash in the ankle-
deep water of the Merced River
or submerge yourself in the chilly
waters of the mountain lakes.
Yosemite has enough options to
satisfy your inner Goldilocks.

Valley Floor Tour: Hop on a tram
for a two-hour tour of Yosemite's
vast and varied landscape, from
granite cliffs to rushing waterfalls.
In winter, the tram is replaced by
a heated motor coach!

Park *in* Numbers

232
Area covered (sq miles)

6,508
Height of Observation Point (ft)

78+
Species of mammals

63

UT

ZION NATIONAL PARK

Waltz into a fairy tale at Zion, where sandstone walls shape themselves into castles, battlements, and narrow passageways. Take a quest to see the canyon in all its glory. Its majestic, wide-open arena seems to beg for a dragon.

*L*ike so many epic adventures, this journey begins with a portal. At Zion, the magic entrance is a dark tunnel carved into a thick, sandstone wall. You emerge suddenly into a shock of light. Red rock walls curve up and around you. Some corridors squeeze tight, as if trying to wrap you in a geologic hug. Welcome!

📷 *Main images: Kanarra Creek slot canyon trail (below); view over a cliff (top right); bighorn sheep (bottom right). Snapshots left to right: Rock formations; path to Angels Landing; Zion Canyon from Angels Landing.*

Two hundred forty million years ago, the soaring red rock cliffs were humble sand dunes—but Earth had other plans. After a turbulent period of geologic rumblings shot the ground upward, the Virgin River began to carve the canyon and its winding narrows. Now that the tectonic turbulence has ended, wildlife flock and flutter in Zion Canyon. Guarded by the sheer walls of the Navajo Sandstone, the tranquil valley is a refuge for hundreds of animal species, which also find peace in Zion's hanging gardens and many ponds.

The park is also a haven for a very different type of creature—the outdoor adventurer. There is plenty of excitement to be found in its skinny slot canyons and dizzying cliffs. Millions of visitors try their hand at canyoneering and hiking, from the winding Narrows to Angels Landing. Climb on!

THINGS to SEE

Arizona Toads: You might hear these toads before you spot them. The males' high-pitched mating calls last for about six seconds. Hope you like love songs!

Piñon Pines: You've probably eaten these trees' highly nutritious edible nuts without even knowing it. Late bloomers, piñons can take up to 80 years to grow 10 feet.

THINGS to DO

Temple of Sinawava: This easy-to-hike trail leads straight to the Narrows. If you don't want to navigate the maze of natural passageways, you can enjoy the view of the Great White Throne!

Ride the Shuttle: *Chug-chug-chug* through Zion's magnificent sights on the free tram, which has shuttled millions of visitors into the canyon. Hop on and off as you please.

Arid: Dry or barren, specifically from having received little rainfall

Ash flow: The extremely hot rock fragments, gas, and other earthen materials that spew from overheated volcanoes

Biodiversity: The variety of life, specifically the number of animal and plant species, within an ecosystem or habitat

Caldera: A large volcanic crater

Conservation: The preservation, restoration, or protection of the natural environment

Ecosystem: An interconnected community of animals, plants, and their physical environment

Endemic: Native to a specific area; found only within a certain limited habitat

Erosion: The process of being worn down by wind, water, or other natural forces

Hoodoo: A naturally occurring column of rock

Hydrothermal: An adjective that describes hot water, usually heated by the earth's crust

Naturalist: A fan or student of or expert in natural history, the history of Earth, the environment, or nature

Old-growth forest: A forest in which most trees have never been cut down or cleared

Prairie: A large, open area of grassland

Strata: Layers of rock

Tundra: A large, flat, treeless region in which the soil is permanently frozen

INDEX

IMAGE CREDITS

Illustration © 2019, 2024 Mike Lowery

Front cover: Richard Mitchell - Touching Light Photography/Getty Images (Mt. Rainier) / **Back cover:** Stephen Moehle/500px (Grand Canyon); Stacy McCormack/500px (Denali); Aaron M/500px (Yosemite) / **2-3:** Cvijovic Zarko/Shutterstock (map) / **4:** Justin Reznick Photography/Getty Images/Flickr RF / **7:** Mirko Liu/Shutterstock (balanced rock) / **8-9:** Ron and Patty Thomas/Getty Images / **10-11:** Joseph Sohm/Shutterstock (coastline); Raimund Koch/Getty Images (cliffs); decojules1/Budget Travel (sunrise); f11photo/Shutterstock (bridge) / **12-13:** David Kirkland/Design Pics/Getty Images / **14-15:** KatiCorsaut/Budget Travel (beach); Wayne Via/Shutterstock (Fatu Rock); Placebo365/Getty Images (coral); BlueBarronPhoto/Getty Images (Samoan fruit bat); photosync/ Shutterstock (snorkel) / **16-17:** wizardofwonders/Shutterstock / **18-19:** Colin D. Young/Shutterstock (Delicate Arch); Rusty Dodson (rattlesnake); anthony heflin/Shutterstock (Turret Arch); Delpixel/Shutterstock (petroglyphs); muha04 (arches); Brad McGinley Photography/Getty Images (arches) / **20-21:** Andrew Nay/ EyeEm/Getty Images / **22-23:** Mark Read/Lonely Planet (rock formations); BlueBarronPhoto/Shutterstock (Milky Way); Teri Virbickis/Shutterstock (bighorn sheep); Gary L. Miller/Shutterstock (turkey vulture) / **24-25:** Denis Jr. Tangney/Getty Images / **26-27:** T photography/Shutterstock (Rio Grande); Fred LaBounty/Shutterstock (post office); Oleg Moiseyenko/Getty Images (yucca tree); Henryk Sadura/Shutterstock (coyote) / **28-29:** Fotoluminate LLC/Shutterstock / **30-31:** Arend Trent/Shutterstock (lighthouse); Jeff Stamer/Shutterstock (manatee); Stephen Frink/Getty Images (spoonbills); Pupes/Shutterstock (canoe) / **32-33:** Patrick Lienin/Getty Images / **34-35:** AlexeyKamenskiy/Getty Images/iStockphoto (canyon); Dan Giveon/Shutterstock (chipmunk); Alexey Kamenskiy/ Shutterstock (juniper tree) / **36-37:** William Hocking/500px (canyon) / **38-39:** MightyPix/Shutterstock (canyon); James Marvin Phelps/Shutterstock (prairie dog); William Hocking/500px (canyon); Daniel Viñé Garcia/Getty Images (Milky Way); b_b_bella/Shutterstock (pine cone); fotoVoyager/Getty Images (Paunsaugunt Plateau) / **40-41:** Matteo Colombo/Getty Images / **42-43:** Kris Wiktor/Shutterstock (Milky Way); Anton Foltin/Shutterstock (spires); Scott Prokop/Shutterstock (Colorado River); fabio simonetto/Shutterstock (Canyonlands); Jeff R Clow/Getty Images/Moment RF (Mesa Arch); Peter Wey/Shutterstock (petroglyphs); Jana Mackova/Shutterstock (kangaroo rat) / **44-45:** pabradyphoto/Getty Images / **46-47:** mpagano/Budget Travel (Route 24); Johnny Adolphson/Shutterstock (barn); Gary Samples/Getty Images/Flickr Open (golden eagle) / **48-49:** Design Pics/Getty Images / **50-51:** Doug Meek/Shutterstock (columns); James Ronan/EyeEm/Getty Images (cave entrance); Sementer/Shutterstock (bat); Mikhail Gnatkovskiy/Shutterstock (centipede) / **52-53:** Tomas Tichy/Shutterstock / **54-55:** Andre Nantel/Shutterstock (pierced rock); David Osborn/Shutterstock (elephant seal); Douglas Klug/ Getty Images (sea lion); Douglas Klug/Getty Images (anemone); Bill Perry/Shutterstock (cactus); Kyle T Perry/ Shutterstock (island fox); Bram Reusen/Shutterstock (Santa Cruz) / **56-57:** Sungjin Ahn Photography/Getty Images / **58-59:** Jimmy Gray Photo/Shutterstock (boardwalk); JamesKarner/Getty Images (swampland); flashbacknyc/Shutterstock (spider); WiP-Studio/Shutterstock (oar); Glenn Ross Images/Getty Images (fungi); Denton Rumsey/Shutterstock (rotting cyprus) / **60-61:** Joshua Huber/Getty Images / **62-63:** Tom Schwabel/Getty Images (Wizard Island); Bill45/Shutterstock (Phantom Ship Island); Southern Lightscapes-Australia/Getty Images (cliffs); Barna Tanko/Shutterstock (snowshoes) / **64-65:** fdastudillo/Getty Images/iStockphoto / **66-67:** Howard Grill/Getty Images/Moment RF (Blue Hen Falls); outdoorimages/Shutterstock (bridge); Kenneth Keifer/Shutterstock (Everett Covered Bridge); David Watkins/Shutterstock (goose) / **68-69:** Doug Meek/Shutterstock / **70-71:** Sylvia Bentele Fotografie/Shutterstock (Zabriskie Point); Efrain Padro/Alamy Stock Photo (Telescope Peak); billybruce2000/Shutterstock (bighorn sheep); George Aldridge/Shutterstock (burros); Sarah Fields Photography/Shutterstock (flowers) / **72-73:** Stacy McCormack/500px / **74-75:** Michael Heffernan/Lonely Planet (Denali); Jacob W. Frank/Getty Images/Flickr RF (grizzly bear); Gary Schultz/Design Pics/Getty Images/Design Pics RF (Dall sheep); Daniel A. Leifheit/Getty Images (caribou) / **76-77:** Boogich/Getty Images / **78-79:** Matt Munro/Lonely Planet (moat); Tatagatta/Getty Images (cannon); Boogich/Getty Images (crab); Posnov/Getty Images (lower archways) / **80-81:** Andy Ross/EyeEm/Getty Images / **82-83:** Andy Lidstone/Shutterstock (boardwalk); Chantal Cecchetti/500px (alligator); Smileus/iStock/Getty Images (flamingos); Audrey R. Smith/ Shutterstock (butterfly orchid); Romrodphoto/Shutterstock (wetland) / **84-85:** Design Pics Inc/Alamy Stock Photo / **86-87:** Menno Schaefer/Shutterstock (Sukakpak Mountain); Scott Dickerson/Design Pics/Getty Images (wolf tracks); Jérémie LeBlond-Fontaine/Getty Images (owl) / **88-89:** STLJB/Shutterstock / **91:** f11photo/ Shutterstock / **92-93:** LeonWang/Shutterstock (bald eagle); photomaster/Shutterstock (bison); Agami Photo Agency/Shutterstock (condor); AYImages/Getty Images (wolf); Jason Patrick Ross (salamander); USFWS Photo (Kentucky cave shrimp); USFWS Photo (pupfish) / **94-95:** ramesh iyanswamy/500px / **96-97:** puttsk/Shutterstock (St. Mary Lake); Posnov/Getty Images/Moment RF (mountain goat); outdoorsman/Shutterstock (lynx); Jérémie LeBlond-Fontaine / **98-99:** Maridav/Shutterstock / **100-101:** Betty Wiley/Getty Images/Moment RF (humpback whale); Benny Marty/Shutterstock (Glacier Bay); Menno Schaefer/Shutterstock (sea otter) / **102-103:** Dean Fikar/Getty Images / **104-105:** Stephen Moehle/500px (Grand Canyon); George Lamson/Shutterstock (condor); Sapna Reddy Photography/Getty Images (watchtower); ronnybas/Shutterstock (Havasu Falls) / **106-107:** Skreidzeleu/Shutterstock (Horseshoe Bend); laminarwind/Budget Travel (cliffs); Fredlyfish4/Shutterstock (Phantom Ranch); FilippoBacci/Getty Images (sunrise); Steven Love/Getty Images (Dark-Eyed Junco) / **108-109:** Mattias Lindstroem/500px / **110-111:** Ferran Traite Soler/Getty Images/iStockphoto (Hidden Falls); Ken Canning/Getty Images (barn); Paul Tessier/Shutterstock (pronghorn); Dean Fikar/Getty Images/Flickr RF (flowers); Mark Read/Lonely Planet (horses) / **112-113:** Rachid Dahnoun/Getty Images / **114-115:** Arlene Treiber Waller (Wheeler Park); IrinaK/Shutterstock (Lehman Caves); Gromit702/Getty Images (Milky Way); Dennis W Donohue/Shutterstock (horses) / **116-117:** Mike Berenson/Colorado Captures/Getty Images / **118-119:** Rosalie Kreulen/Shutterstock (sunrise); Viktor Loki/Shutterstock (toad); Galyna Andrushko/Shutterstock (dunes) / **120-121:** Sean Pavone/Getty Images/iStockphoto / **122-123:** Dean Fikar/Shutterstock (mist); IrinaK/Shutterstock (Tom Branch Falls); jadimages/Shutterstock (black bear); Gabbie Berry/Shutterstock (salamander) / **124-125:** Inge Johnsson/Alamy Stock Photo / **126-127:** Wildnerdpix/Shutterstock (Devil's Hall); Victoria "Tori" Meyer/ Shutterstock (Guadalupe Mountains); Richard A McMillin/Shutterstock (cypress tree); Deep Desert Photography/Shutterstock (jackrabbit) / **128-129:** Westend61/Getty Images / **130-131:** Michele Falzone/Getty Images (Oheo Gulch); topseller/Shutterstock (volcano crater); Vlue/Shutterstock (volcanic landscape) / **132-133:** Jo Crebbin/Shutterstock / **134-135:** Tan Yilmaz/Getty Images (waterfall); lovu4ever/Shutterstock (honeycreeper); Luc Kohnen/Shutterstock (gecko); Andre Nantel/Shutterstock (Thurston Lava Tube); MNStudio/ Shutterstock (Kilauea Iki trail); Bryan Busovicki/Shutterstock (lava skylight) / **136-137:** Zack Frank/Shutterstock / **138-139:** Bram Reusen/Shutterstock (cascades); Zack Frank/Shutterstock (trail); Jeremy Janus Photography/ Shutterstock (wilderness); All Stock Photos/Shutterstock (mineral hot water) / **140-141:** ehrlif/Shutterstock (beach) / **142-143:** photo.eccles/Shutterstock (lighthouse beach); Single-Tooth Productions/Getty Images (dunes); Kelly vanDellen/Shutterstock (forest floor); Ray Hennessy/Shutterstock (warbler) / **144-145:** StevenSchremp/Getty Images/iStockphoto (lighthouse) / **146-147:** Ana Gram/Shutterstock (wolf); Posnov/Getty Images/Moment Open (Rock Harbor); Geoffrey George/Getty Images (Shaw Island) / **148-149:** Christian Reister/ Mauritius images GmbH/Alamy Stock Photo (Joshua Tree) / **150-151:** Dennis W Donohue/Shutterstock (roadrunner); S.Borisov/Shutterstock (landscape); Marisa Estivill/Shutterstock (Cholla Cactus Garden); Matteo Colombo/Getty Images (rock formation); Runa0410/Shutterstock (Joshua tree) / **152-153:** Feng Wei Photography/Getty Images (Alaska coastline) / **154-155:** Santiparp Wattanaporn/Shutterstock (sea lions); Chase Dekker/Shutterstock (brown bear); Gleb Tarro/ Shutterstock (grizzly bear family); Bildagentur Zoonar GmbH (coastline) / **156-157:** Tomasz Wozniak/Shutterstock (Spire Cove) / **158-159:** Westend61 Premium/Shutterstock (Resurrection Bay); Steven Schremp/Shutterstock (coastline Alaska); CSNafzger/Shutterstock (puffin); reisegraf.ch/Shutterstock (Exit Glacier); davidhoffmann photography/Shutterstock (orca whale); BlueBarronPhoto/Shutterstock (seal) / **160-161:** Chiara Salvadori/Getty Images (Kings Canyon) / **162-163:** Sierraiara/Getty (Kings Canyon); Susan Kehoe/Shutterstock (black bear cub); Leene/Shutterstock (Kings River) / **164-165:** BlueBarronPhoto/Getty Images (Kobuk Valley) / **166-167:** Jukka Jantunen/Shutterstock (lynx); Tom Walker/Getty Images (antlers); Tom Walker/Alamy Stock Photo (caribou); John Schwieder/Alamy Stock Photo (caribou on dunes); National

Geographic Image Collection/Alamy Stock Photo (Kobuk Valley) / **168-169:** Ken Baldwin/500px (Lake Clark Alaska) / **170-171:** FloridaStock/Shutterstock (bald eagle); Dennis Blum/Shutterstock (aerial view); Rob Daugherty/Design Pics/Getty Images (grizzly bears); Marc_Latremouille/Getty Images (brown bears); Art Wolfe/Getty Images/Mint Images RF (puffins) / **172-173:** Lucila10/Getty Images (Lassen hydrothermal system) / **174-175:** kojihirano/Getty Images/iStockphoto (Painted Dunes Lassen); Potapov Alexander/ Shutterstock (tortoise-shell butterfly); Tristan Brynildsen/Shutterstock (Lassen Peak); SMcGuire45/Getty Images (Lassen) / **176-177:** Zack Frank/Shutterstock (Mammoth Cave) / **178-179:** Weldon Schloneger/Shutterstock (rock overhang); Zack Frank/Shutterstock (cave entrance); jiawangkun/Shutterstock (cave interior) / **180-181:** Wisanu Boonrawd/Shutterstock (Milky Way); Wisanu Boonrawd/Shutterstock (Balanced Rock); Rommel Canlas/ Shutterstock (Joshua Tree); Benjamin Derge/Wikipedia (foxfire) / **182-183:** www.infinitahighway.com.br/Getty Images (Mesa Verde) / **184-185:** YinYang/Getty Images/iStockphoto (cliff dwelling); Bob Kuo/500px (kiva) / **186-187:** Richard Mitchell - Touching Light Photography/Getty Images (Mt. Rainier) / **188-189:** Kelly vanDellen/ Shutterstock (fox); Checubus/Shutterstock (Sunrise Lake); DonLand/Shutterstock (Narada Falls); Feng Wei Photography/Getty Images/Flickr RF (floral landscape) / **190-191:** Brian Evans/Getty Images/iStockphoto (gorge) / **192-193:** Billy McDonald (Sandstone Falls); Picasa (Virginia bat); Gestalt Imagery (coal tower); Malachi Jacobs (river) / **194-195:** Shane Myers Photography/Shutterstock (North Cascades) / **196-197:** KingWu/Getty Images (Mt. Shuksan); Checubus/Shutterstock (North Cascades); Zuzana Gabrielova/Shutterstock (wolverine); Dec Hogan/Shutterstock (Chinook salmon) / **198-199:** 2009fotofriends/Shutterstock (Olympic National Park) / **200-201:** Westend61/Getty Images (Sol Duc River); Dan Ratliff/Shutterstock (marmot); Ken Canning/Getty Images (deer) / **202-203:** MargaretW/Getty Images (Petrified Forest National Park) / **204-205:** MNStudio/ Shutterstock (canyon); sumikophoto/Shutterstock (petroglyphs); Sean Lema/Shutterstock (petrified wood); Felix Lipov/Shutterstock (petrified wood); Seltiva/Getty Images (lizard) / **206-207:** David Madison (Pinnacles National Park) / **208-209:** yhelfman/Shutterstock (volcanic rock landscape); yhelfman Shutterstock (scrub-jay); Zack Frank/Shutterstock (Pinnacles National Park) / **210-211:** Phillip Bindeman/500px (Redwood National Park) / **212-213:** MNStudio/Shutterstock (Muir forest); Zack Frank/Shutterstock (beach); Kris Wiktor/Shutterstock (Muir Woods) / **214-215:** Crystal Brindle/500px (Rocky Mountain National Park) / **216-217:** mmiwig/Budget Travel (lake); Greg and Jan Ritchie/Shutterstock (bighorn sheep); bjul/Shutterstock (Rocky Mountain National Park); Mike Berenson/Colorado Captures/Getty Images/Moment RF (sunset) / **218-219:** Jay Pierstorff/Getty Images (Saguaro) / **220-221:** Josemaria Toscano/Shutterstock (sunset); Frank Fichtmueller/Shutterstock (javelina); Dmitry Vinogradov/500px (dirt road Saguaro) / **222-223:** Dmitry Vinogradov/500px (sequoia) / **224-225:** Mario A. De Leo Winkler (accrama)/Getty Images/Moment RF (sequoia); Paola Moschitको-Assenmacher/EyeEm/Getty Images/EyeEm (sequoias); lucky-photographer/Alamy Stock Photo (trunk tunnel) / **226-227:** OGphoto/Getty Images (Shenandoah Valley) / **228-229:** Jon Bilous/ Shutterstock (Blue Ridge Mountains); mlorenz/Shutterstock (bobcat); Joseph Gruber/Shutterstock (Shenandoah Valley); Photography by Deb Snelson/Getty Images/Flickr Open (White Oak Canyon) / **230-231:** Comstock Images/Getty Images (Theodore Roosevelt National Park) / **232-233:** ZakZeinert/Shutterstock (Theodore Roosevelt National Park); Nancy Bauer/Shutterstock (prairie dog); Henryk Sadura/Shutterstock (horses) / **234-235:** cdwheatley/Getty Images (Trunk Bay) / **236-237:** Nine OK/Getty Images (Reef Bay); Junior Braz/ Shutterstock (bananaquit); Jo Ann Snover/Shutterstock (Annaberg Plantation); bluepompano/Getty Images (sea stars) / **238-239:** RGB Ventures/SuperStock/Alamy Stock Photo (Voyageurs National Park) / **240-241:** Frank Kennedy MN/Shutterstock (Voyageurs National Park); lffing/Shutterstock (waterfall); Mike Norkum/Shutterstock (loons); BlueBarronPhoto/Shutterstock (northern lights); Jody Ann/Shutterstock (beaver) / **242-243:** ferrantraite/Getty Images (White Sands National Park) / **244-245:** Paul Omernik/Getty Images (bleached earless lizard); National Park Service; NASA / **246-247:** Zachary Frank/Alamy Stock Photo (Wind Cave) / **248-249:** All Canada Photos/Alamy Stock Photo (bison herd); Zack Frank/Shutterstock (boxwork rock formation); Jacob Boomsma/Shutterstock (Wind Cave tunnel); Kerry Hargrove/Shutterstock (ferret); Zack Frank/ Shutterstock (Wind Cave) / **250-251:** Frans Lanting/Getty Images/Mint Images (Wrangell-St. Elias National Park) / **252-253:** Benny Marty/Shutterstock (Wrangell-St. Elias National Park); Troutnut/Shutterstock (sunset) / **254-255:** Feng Wei Photography/Getty Images (Yellowstone) / **256-257:** Mark Read/Lonely Planet (bison); BGSmith/ Shutterstock (grizzly bear); Matt Munro/Lonely Planet (Lower Yellowstone Falls); kwiktor/Getty Images/ iStockphoto (Grand Prismatic Spring) / **258-259:** Martin Ruegner/Getty Images/Radius Images (Old Faithful); Jim Cumming/Shutterstock (wolves) / **260-261:** Aaron M/500px (Yosemite) / **262-263:** Piriya Photography/Getty Images (Half Dome); Kaori Tanabe/Getty Images/Moment RF (Yosemite); Eric Dale/Shutterstock (marmot); Anna Gorin/Getty Images (Vernal Falls) / **264-265:** Peter Kunasz/ Shutterstock (Zion) / **266-267:** kan_khampanya/ Shutterstock (Kanarra Creek); Bartfett/Getty Images (cliff); Alaskaphoto/Shutterstock (bighorn sheep); Aaron Meyers/Getty Images/Flickr RF (rock formations); Frank Bach/Shutterstock (cliff path); Kevin Crowley/500px (Zion Canyon)

ACKNOWLEDGEMENTS

Publishing Director: Piers Pickard / **Publisher:** Rebecca Hunt / **Editor:** Rhoda Belleza and Priyanka Lamichhane / **Author:** Alexa Ward / **Illustrator:** Mike Lowery / **Art Director:** Andrew Mansfield **Print Production:** Nigel Longuet

Published in May 2024 by Lonely Planet Global Limited / CRN: 554153 / ISBN: 978 1 83758 258 7 www.lonelyplanet.com/kids / © Lonely Planet 2024 / 10 9 8 7 6 5 4 3 2 1 Printed in China

STAY IN TOUCH - lonelyplanet.com/contact

Lonely Planet Office:
IRELAND
Digital Depot, Roe Lane (off Thomas St), Digital Hub, Dublin 8, D08 TCV4, Ireland